Walker's Appeal

In Four Articles

David Walker

APPLEWOOD BOOKS
Bedford, Massachusetts

Walker's Appeal
was originally published in

1830

ISBN: 978-1-4290-1636-0

Thank you for purchasing an Applewood book. Applewood reprints America's lively classics—books from the past that are still of interest to modern readers. This facsimile was printed using many new technologies together to bring our tradition-bound mission to you. Applewood's facsimile edition of this work may include library stamps, scribbles, and margin notes as they exist in the original book. These interesting historical artifacts celebrate the place the book was read or the person who read the book. In addition to these artifacts, the work may have additional errors that were either in the original, in the digital scans, or introduced as we prepared the book for printing. If you believe the work has such errors, please let us know by writing to us at the address below.

For a free copy of our current print catalog featuring our bestselling book, write to:

APPLEWOOD BOOKS
PO Box 365
Bedford, MA 01730

For more complete listings, visit us on the web at:
awb.com

Prepared for publishing by HP

WALKER'S

APPEAL,

IN FOUR ARTICLES;

TOGETHER WITH

A PREAMBLE,

TO THE

COLOURED CITIZENS OF THE WORLD,

BUT IN PARTICULAR, AND VERY EXPRESSLY, TO THOSE OF

THE UNITED STATES OF AMERICA,

WRITTEN IN BOSTON, STATE OF MASSACHUSETTS,
SEPTEMBER 28, 1829.

THIRD AND LAST EDITION,
WITH ADDITIONAL NOTES, CORRECTIONS, &c.

Boston:
REVISED AND PUBLISHED BY DAVID WALKER.
....
1830.

☞ It will be recollected, that I, in the first edition of my " Appeal,"* promised to demonstrate in the course of which, viz. in the course of my Appeal, to the satisfaction of the most incredulous mind, that we Coloured People of these United States, are, the most wretched, degraded and abject set of beings that ever lived since the world began, down to the present day, and, that, the white Christians of America, who hold us in slavery, (or, more properly speaking, pretenders to Christianity,) treat us more cruel and barbarous than any Heathen nation did any people whom it had subjected, or reduced to the same condition, that the Americans (who are, notwithstanding, looking for the Millennial day) have us. All I ask is, for a candid and careful perusal of this the third and last edition of my Appeal, where the world may see that we, the Blacks or Coloured People, are treated more cruel by the white Christians of America, than devils themselves ever treated a set of men, women and children on this earth.☜

☞ It is expected that all coloured men, women and children,† of every nation, language and tongue under heaven, will try to procure a copy of this Appeal and read it, or get some one to read it to them, for it is designed more particularly for them. Let them remember, that though our cruel oppressors and murderers, may (if possible) treat us more cruel, as Pharoah did the children of Israel, yet the God of the Etheopeans, has been pleased to hear our moans in consequence of oppression; and the day of our redemption from abject wretchedness draweth near, when we shall be enabled, in the most extended sense of the word, to stretch forth our hands to the LORD our GOD, but there must be a willingness on our part, for GOD to do these things for us, for we may be assured that he will not take us by the hairs of our head against our will and desire, and drag us from our very, mean, low and abject condition.☜

*See my Preamble in first edtition, first page. See also 2d edition, Article 1, page 9.

† Who are not too deceitful, abject, and servile to resist the cruelties and murders inflicted upon us by the white slave holders, our enemies by nature.

APPEAL, &c.

PREAMBLE.

My dearly beloved Brethren and Fellow Citizens.

HAVING travelled over a considerable portion of these United States, and having, in the course of my travels, taken the most accurate observations of things as they exist—the result of my observations has warranted the full and unshaken conviction, that we, (coloured people of these United States,) are the most degraded, wretched, and abject set of beings that ever lived since the world began; and I pray God that none like us ever may live again until time shall be no more. They tell us of the Israelites in Egypt, the Helots in Sparta, and of the Roman Slaves, which last were made up from almost every nation under heaven, whose sufferings under those ancient and heathen nations, were, in comparison with ours, under this enlightened and Christian nation, no more than a cypher—or, in other words, those heathen nations of antiquity, had but little more among them than the name and form of slavery; while wretchedness and endless miseries were reserved, apparently in a phial, to be poured out upon our fathers, ourselves and our children, by *Christian* Americans!

These positions I shall endeavour, by the help of the Lord, to demonstrate in the course of this *Appeal,* to the satisfaction of the most incredulous mind—and may God Almighty, who is the Father of our Lord Jesus Christ, open your hearts to understand and believe the truth.

The *causes,* my brethren, which produce our wretchedness and miseries, are so very numerous and aggravating, that I believe the pen only of a Josephus or a Plutarch, can well enumerate and explain them. Upon subjects, then, of such incompre-

hensible magnitude, so impenetrable, and so notorious, I shall be obliged to omit a large class of, and
content myself with giving you an exposition of a
few of those, which do indeed rage to such an alarm-
ing pitch, that they cannot but be a perpetual source
of terror and dismay to every reflecting mind.

I am fully aware, in making this appeal to my
much afflicted and suffering brethren, that I shall
not only be assailed by those whose greatest earthly desires are, to keep us in abject ignorance and
wretchedness, and who are of the firm conviction
that Heaven has designed us and our children to be
slaves and *beasts of burden* to them and their children.   I say, I do not only expect to be held up to
the public as an ignorant, impudent and restless dis-
turber of the public peace, by such avaricious creatures, as well as a mover of insubordination—and
perhaps put in prison or to death, for giving a superfi-
cial exposition of our miseries, and exposing tyrants.
But I am persuaded, that many of my brethren, particularly those who are ignorantly in league with
slave-holders or tyrants, who acquire their daily
bread by the blood and sweat of their more ignorant
brethren—and not a few of those too, who are too
ignorant to see an inch beyond their noses, will rise
up and call me cursed—Yea, the jealous ones among
us will perhaps use more abject subtlety, by affirm-
ing that this work is not worth perusing , that we
are well situated, and there is no use in trying to
better our condition, for we cannot.   I will ask one
question here.—Can our condition be any worse?—
Can it be more mean and abject? If there are any
changes, will they not be for the better, though they
may appear for the worst at first? Can they get us
any lower? Where can they get us? They are
afraid to treat us worse, for they know well, the day
they do it they are gone.   But against all accusa-
tions which may or can be preferred against me, I
appeal to Heaven for my motive in writing—who
knows that my object is, if possible, to awaken in

the breasts of my afflicted, degraded and slumbering brethren, a spirit of inquiry and investigation respecting our miseries and wretchedness in this *Republican Land of Liberty ! ! ! ! ! !*

The sources from which our miseries are derived, and on which I shall comment, I shall not combine in one, but shall put them under distinct heads and expose them in their turn ; in doing which, keeping truth on my side, and not departing from the strictest rules of morality, I shall endeavour to penetrate, search out, and lay them open for your inspection. If you cannot or will not profit by them, I shall have done *my* duty to you, my country and my God.

And as the inhuman system of *slavery*, is the *source* from which most of our miseries proceed, I shall begin with that *curse to nations*, which has spread terror and devastation through so many nations of antiquity, and which is raging to such a pitch at the present day in Spain and in Portugal. It had one tug in England, in France, and in the United States of America ; yet the inhabitants thereof, do not learn wisdom, and erase it entirely from their dwellings and from all with whom they have to do. The fact is, the labour of slaves comes so cheap to the avaricious usurpers, and is (as they think) of such great utility to the country where it exists, that those who are actuated by sordid avarice only, overlook the evils, which will as sure as the Lord lives, follow after the good. In fact, they are so happy to keep in ignorance and degradation, and to receive the homage and the labour of the slaves, they forget that God rules in the armies of heaven and among the inhabitants of the earth, having his ears continually open to the cries, tears and groans of his oppressed people ; and being a just and holy Being will at one day appear fully in behalf of the oppressed, and arrest the progress of the avaricious oppressors ; for although the destruction of the oppressors God may not effect by the oppressed, yet the Lord our God will bring other destructions upon them—for not

unfrequently will he cause them to rise up one
against another, to be split and divided, and to oppress each other, and sometimes to open hostilities
with sword in hand.   Some may ask, what is the
matter with this united and happy people?—Some
say it is the cause of political usurpers, tyrants, oppressors, &c.   But has not the Lord an oppressed
and suffering people among them?   Does the Lord
condescend to hear their cries and see their tears
in consequence of oppression?   Will he let the oppressors rest comfortably and happy always?   Will
he not cause the very children of the oppressors to
rise up against them, and oftimes put them to death?
" God works in many ways his wonders to perform."

I will not here speak of the destructions which
the Lord brought upon Egypt, in consequence of
the oppression and consequent groans of the oppressed—of the hundreds and thousands of Egyptians whom God hurled into the Red Sea for afflicting his people in their land—of the Lord's suffering
people in Sparta or Lacedemon, the land of the truly
famous Lycurgus—nor have I time to comment upon
the cause which produced the fierceness with which
Sylla usurped the title, and absolutely acted as dic-
tator of the Roman people—the conspiracy of Cat-
aline—the conspiracy against, and murder of Cæsar
in the Senate house—the spirit with which Marc
Antony made himself master of the commonwealth
—his associating Octavius and Lipidus with himself
in power—their dividing the provinces of Rome
among themselves—their attack and defeat, on the
plains of Phillippi, of the last defenders of their liberty, (Brutus and Cassius)—the tyranny of Tibe-
rius, and from him to the final overthrow of Con-
stantinople by the Turkish Sultan, Mahomed II.
A. D. 1453.   I say, I shall not take up time to
speak of the *causes* which produced so much wretchedness and massacre among those heathen nations,
for I am aware that you know too well, that God is

just, as well as merciful !—I shall call your attention a
few moments to that *Christian* nation, the Spaniards
—while I shall leave almost unnoticed, that avaricious and cruel people, the Portuguese, among
whom all true hearted Christians and lovers of Jesus
Christ, must evidently see the judgments of God
displayed.   To show the judgments of God upon
the Spaniards, I shall occupy but a little time, leaving a plenty of room for the candid and unprejudiced to reflect.

All persons who are acquainted with history, and
particularly the Bible, who are not blinded by the
God of this world, and are not actuated solely by
avarice—who are able to lay aside prejudice long
enough to view candidly and impartially, things as
they were, are, and probably will be—who are willing to admit that God made man to serve Him *alone*,
and that man should have no other Lord or Lords
but Himself—that God Almighty is the *sole proprie-
tor* or *master* of the WHOLE human family, and will
not on any consideration admit of a colleague, being unwilling to divide his glory with another—
and who can dispense with prejudice long enough
to admit that we are *men*, notwithstanding our *im-
prominent noses* and *woolly heads*, and believe that we
feel for our fathers, mothers, wives and children,
as well as the whites do for theirs.—I say, all who are
permitted to see and believe these things, can easily
recognize the judgments of God among the Spaniards.   Though others may lay the cause of the
fierceness with which they cut each other's throats,
to some other circumstance, yet they who believe
that God is a God of justice, will believe that
SLAVERY *is the principal cause.*

While the Spaniards are running about upon the
field of battle cutting each other's throats, has not
the Lord an afflicted and suffering people in the
midst of them, whose cries and groans in consequence
of oppression are continually pouring into the ears
of the God of justice? Would they not cease to cut

each other's throats, if they could? But how can they? The very support which they draw from government to aid them in perpetrating such enormities, does it not arise in a great degree from the wretched victims of oppression among them? And yet they are calling for *Peace!—Peace!!* Will any peace be given unto them? Their destruction may indeed be procrastinated awhile, but can it continue long, while they are oppressing the Lord's people? Has He not the hearts of all men in His hand? Will he suffer one part of his creatures to go on oppressing another like brutes always, with impunity? And yet, those avaricious wretches are calling for *Peace!!!!* I declare, it does appear to me, as though some nations think God is asleep, or that he made the Africans for nothing else but to dig their mines and work their farms, or they cannot believe history, sacred or profane. I ask every man who has a heart, and is blessed with the privilege of believing—Is not God a God of justice to *all* his creatures? Do you say he is? Then if he gives peace and tranquillity to tyrants, and permits them to keep our fathers, our mothers, ourselves and our children in eternal ignorance and wretchedness, to support them and their families, would he be to us a God of *justice?* I ask, O ye *Christians!!!* who hold us and our children in the most abject ignorance and degradation, that ever a people were afflicted with since the world began—I say, if God gives you peace and tranquillity, and suffers you thus to go on afflicting us, and our children, who have never given you the least provocation—would he be to us *a God of justice?* If you will allow that we are MEN, who feel for each other, does not the blood of our fathers and of us their children, cry aloud to the Lord of Sabaoth against you, for the cruelties and murders with which you have, and do continue to afflict us. But it is time for me to close my remarks on the suburbs, just to enter more fully into the interior of this system of cruelty and oppression.

ARTICLE I.

OUR WRETCHEDNESS IN CONSEQUENCE OF SLAVERY.

My beloved brethren:—The Indians of North and of South America—the Greeks—the Irish, subjected under the king of Great Britain—the Jews, that ancient people of the Lord—the inhabitants of the islands of the sea—in fine, all the inhabitants of the earth, (except however, the sons of Africa) are called *men*, and of course are, and ought to be free. But we, (coloured people) and our children are *brutes !!* and of course are, and *ought to be* SLAVES to the American people and their children forever ! ! to dig their mines and work their farms; and thus go on enriching them, from one generation to another with our *blood* and our *tears ! ! ! !*

I promised in a preceding page to demonstrate to the satisfaction of the most incredulous, that we, (coloured people of these United States of America) are the *most wretched, degraded* and *abject* set of beings that *ever lived* since the world began, and that the white Americans having reduced us to the wretched state of *slavery,* treat us in that condition *more cruel* (they being an enlighted and Christian people,) than any heathen nation did any people whom it had reduced to our condition. These affirmations are so well confirmed in the minds of all unprejudiced men, who have taken the trouble to read histories, that they need no elucidation from me. But to put them beyond all doubt, I refer you in the first place to the children of Jacob, or of Israel in Egypt, under Pharaoh and his people. Some of my brethren do not know who Pharaoh and the Egyptians were—I know it to be a fact, that some of them take the Egyptians to have been a gang of *devils,* not knowing any better, and that they (Egyptians) having got possession of the Lord's people, treated them *nearly* as cruel as *Christian*

2

Americans do us, at the present day. For the information of such, I would only mention that the Egyptians, were Africans or coloured people, such as we are—some of them yellow and others dark— a mixture of Ethiopians and the natives of Egypt— about the same as you see the coloured people of the United States at the present day.—I say, I call your attention then, to the children of Jacob, while I point out particularly to you his son Joseph, among the rest, in Egypt.

"And Pharaoh, said unto Joseph, thou shalt be "over my house, and according unto thy word "shall all my people be ruled: only in the throne "will I be greater than thou."*

"And Pharaoh said unto Joseph, see, I have set "thee over all the land of Egypt."†

"And Pharaoh said unto Joseph, I am Pharaoh, "and without thee shall no man lift up his hand or "foot in all the land of Egypt."‡

Now I appeal to heaven and to earth, and particularly to the American people themselves, who cease not to declare that our condition is not *hard*, and that we are comparatively satisfied to rest in wretchedness and misery, under them and their children. Not, indeed, to show me a coloured President, a Governor, a Legislator, a Senator, a Mayor, or an Attorney at the Bar.—But to show me a man of colour, who holds the low office of a Constable, or one who sits in a Juror Box, even on a case of one of his wretched brethren, throughout this great Republic ! !—But let us pass Joseph the son of Israel a little farther in review, as he existed with that heathen nation.

"And Pharaoh called Joseph's name Zaphnath- "paaneah; and he gave him to wife Asenath the "daughter of Potipherah priest of On. And Joseph "went out over all the land of Egypt."§

Compare the above, with the American institutions. Do they not institute laws to prohibit us from

* See Genesis, chap. xli.   † xli. 44.   § xli. 45,

marrying among the whites? I would wish, candidly, however, before the Lord, to be understood, that I would not give a *pinch of snuff* to be married to any white person I ever saw in all the days of my life. And I do say it, that the black man, or man of colour, who will leave his own colour (provided he can get one, who is good for any thing) and marry a white woman, to be a double slave to her, just because she is *white*, ought to be treated by her as he surely will be, viz: as a NIGER!!!! It is not, indeed, what I care about inter-marriages with the whites, which induced me to pass this subject in review; for the Lord knows, that there is a day coming when they will be glad enough to get into the company of the blacks, notwithstanding, we are, in this generation, levelled by them, almost on a level with the brute creation: and some of us they treat even worse than they do the brutes that perish. I only made this extract to show how much lower we are held, and how much more cruel we are treated by the Americans, than were the children of Jacob, by the Egyptians.—We will notice the sufferings of Israel some further, under *heathen Pharaoh*, compared with ours under the *enlightened Christians of America.*

"And Pharaoh spake unto Joseph, saying, thy "father and thy brethren are come unto thee:"

"The land of Egypt is before thee: in the best "of the land make thy father and brethren to dwell; "in the land of Goshen let them dwell: and if thou "knowest any men of activity among them, then "make them rulers over my cattle."*

I ask those people who treat us so *well*, Oh! I ask them, where is the most barren spot of land which they have given unto us? Israel had the most fertile land in all Egypt. Need I mention the very notorious fact, that I have known a poor man of colour, who laboured night and day, to acquire a little money, and having acquired it, he vested it in a small piece of land, and got him a house erected

---

* Genesis, chap. xlvii. 5. 6.

thereon, and having paid for the whole, he moved his family into it, where he was suffered to remain but nine months, when he was cheated out of his property by a white man, and driven out of door! And is not this the case generally? Can a man of colour buy a piece of land and keep it peaceably? Will not some white man try to get it from him, even if it is in a *mud hole?* I need not comment any farther on a subject, which all, both black and white, will readily admit. But I must, really, observe that in this very city, when a man of colour dies, if he owned any real estate it most generally falls into the hands of some white person. The wife and children of the deceased may weep and lament if they please, but the estate will be kept snug enough by its white possessor.

But to prove farther that the condition of the Israelites was better under the Egyptians than ours is under the whites. I call upon the professing Christians, I call upon the philanthropist, I call upon the very tyrant himself, to show me a page of history, either sacred or profane, on which a verse can be found, which maintains, that the Egyptians heaped the *insupportable insult* upon the children of Israel, by telling them that they were not of the *human family.* Can the whites deny this charge? Have they not, after having reduced us to the deplorable condition of slaves under their feet, held us up as descending originally from the tribes of *Monkeys* or *Orang-Outangs?* O! my God! I appeal to every man of feeling—is not this insupportable? Is it not heaping the most gross insult upon our miseries, because they have got us under their feet and we cannot help ourselves? Oh! pity us we pray thee, Lord Jesus, Master.—Has Mr. Jefferson declared to the world, that we are inferior to the whites, both in the endowments of our bodies and of minds? It is indeed surprising, that a man of such great learning, combined with such excellent natural parts, should speak so of a set of men in chains. I do not know what to compare it to, unless, like putting one wild deer in an iron cage, where it will be secured, and hold another by the side of the same, then let it go, and expect the one in the cage to run as fast as the one at liberty. So far, my brethren, were the Egyptians from heaping these insults upon their slaves, that Pharoah's daughter took Moses, a son of Israel for her own, as will appear by the following.

" And Pharoah's daughter said unto her, [Moses' " mother] take this child away, and nurse it for me, " and I will pay thee thy wages. And the woman " took the child [Moses] and nursed it.

" And the child grew, and she brought him unto " Pharoah's daughter and he became her son. And " she called his name Moses : and she said because " I drew him out of the water."*

In all probability, Moses would have become Prince Regent to the throne, and no doubt, in process of time but he would have been seated on the throne of Egypt. But he had rather suffer shame, with the people of God, than to enjoy pleasures with that wicked people for a season. O ! that the coloured people were long since of Moses' excellent disposition, instead of courting favour with, and telling news and lies to our *natural enemies*, against each other—aiding them to keep their hellish chains of slavery upon us. Would we not long before this time, have been respectable men, instead of such wretched victims of oppression as we are? Would they be able to drag our mothers, our fathers, our wives, our children and ourselves, around the world in chains and hand-cuffs as they do, to dig up gold and silver for them and theirs? This question, my brethren, I leave for you to digest; and may God Almighty force it home to your hearts. Remember that unless you are united, keeping your tongues within your teeth, you will be afraid to trust your secrets to each other, and thus perpetuate our miseries under the *Christians ! ! ! ! !* ☞ ADDITION.—

---

* See Exodus, chap. ii. 9, 10.

Remember, also to lay humble at the feet of our Lord and Master Jesus Christ, with prayers and fastings. Let our enemies go on with their butcheries, and at once fill up their cup. Never make an attempt to gain our freedom or *natural right*, from under our cruel oppressors and murderers, until you see your way clear*—when that hour arrives and you move, be not afraid or dismayed; for be you assured that Jesus Christ the King of heaven and of earth who is the God of justice and of armies, will surely go before you. And those enemies who have for hundreds of years stolen our *rights*, and kept us ignorant of Him and His divine worship, he will remove. Millions of whom, are this day, so ignorant and avaricious, that they cannot conceive how God can have an attribute of justice, and show mercy to us because it pleased Him to make us black—which colour, Mr. Jefferson calls unfortunate ! ! ! ! ! As though we are not as thankful to our God, for having made us as it pleased himself, as they, (the whites,) are for having made them white. They think because they hold us in their infernal chains of slavery, that we wish to be white, or of their color—but they are dreadfully deceived—we wish to be just as it pleased our Creator to have made us, and no avaricious and unmerciful wretches, have any business to make slaves of, or hold us in slavery. How would they like for us to make slaves of, and hold them in cruel slavery, and murder them as they do us?—

---

* It is not to be understood here, that I mean for us to wait until God shall take us by the hair of our heads and drag us out of abject wretchedness and slavery, nor do I mean to convey the idea for us to wait until our enemies shall make preparations, and call us to seize those preparations, take it away from them, and put every thing before us to death, in order to gain our freedom which God has given us. For you must remember that we are men as well as they. God has been pleased to give us two eyes, two hands, two feet, and some sense in our heads as well as they. They have no more right to hold us in slavery than we have to hold them, we have just as much right, in the sight of God, to hold them and their children in slavery and wretchedness, as they have to hold us, and no more.

But is Mr. Jefferson's assertions true? viz. "that it is unfortunate for us that our Creator has been pleased to make us *black*." We will not take his say so, for the fact. The world will have an opportunity to see whether it is unfortunate for us, that our Creator *has made us* darker than the *whites*.

Fear not the number and education of our *enemies*, against whom we shall have to contend for our lawful right; guaranteed to us by our Maker; for why should we be afraid, when God is, and will continue, (if we continue humble) to be on our side?

The man who would not fight under our Lord and Master Jesus Christ, in the glorious and heavenly cause of freedom and of God—to be delivered from the most wretched, abject and servile slavery, that ever a people was afflicted with since the foundation of the world, to the present day—ought to be kept with all of his children or family, in slavery, or in chains, to be butchered by his *cruel enemies*.

I saw a paragraph, a few years since, in a South Carolina paper, which, speaking of the barbarity of the Turks, it said: "The Turks are the most barbarous people in the world—they treat the Greeks more like *brutes* than human beings." And in the same paper was an advertisement, which said: "Eight well built Virginia and Maryland *Negro fellows* and four *wenches* will positively be *sold this day, to the highest bidder!*" And what astonished me still more was, to see in this same *humane* paper!! the cuts of three men, with clubs and budgets on their backs, and an advertisement offering a considerable sum of money for their apprehension and delivery. I declare, it is really so amusing to hear the Southerners and Westerners of this country talk about *barbarity*, that it is positively, enough to make a man *smile*.

The sufferings of the Helots among the Spartans, were somewhat severe, it is true, but to say that theirs, were as severe as ours among the Americans,

I do most strenuously deny—for instance, can any man show me an article on a page of ancient history which specifies, that, the Spartans chained, and hand-cuffed the Helots, and dragged them from their wives and children, children from their parents, mothers from their suckling babes, wives from their husbands, driving them from one end of the country to the other? Notice the Spartans were heathens, who lived long before our Divine Master made his appearance in the flesh. Can Christian Americans deny these barbarous cruelties? Have you not, Americans, having subjected us under you, added to these miseries, by insulting us in telling us to our face, because we are helpless, that we are not of the human family? I ask you, O! Americans, I ask you, in the name of the Lord, can you deny these charges? Some perhaps may deny, by saying, that they never thought or said that we were not men. But do not actions speak louder than words?—have they not made provisions for the Greeks, and Irish? Nations who have never done the least thing for them, while *we*, who have enriched their country with our blood and tears—have dug up gold and silver for them and their children, from generation to generation, and are in more miseries than any other people under heaven, are not seen, but by comparatively, a handful of the American people? There are indeed, more ways to kill a dog, besides choking it to death with butter. Further—The Spartans or Lacedemonians, had some frivolous pretext, for enslaving the Helots, for they (Helots) while being free inhabitants of Sparta, stirred up an intestine commotion, and were, by the Spartans subdued, and made prisoners of war. Consequently they and their children were condemned to perpetual slavery.*

I have been for years troubling the pages of historians, to find out what our fathers have done to

---

* See Dr. Goldsmith's History of Greece—page 9. See also, Plutarch's Lives. The Helots subdued by Agis, king of *Sparta*.

the *white Christians of America*, to merit such con-
dign punishment as they have inflicted on them, and
do continue to inflict on us their children. But I
must aver, that my researches have hitherto been to
no effect. I have therefore, come to the immoveable conclusion, that they (Americans) have, and do
continue to punish us for nothing else, but for enriching them and their country. For I cannot conceive of any thing else. Nor will I ever believe
otherwise, until the Lord shall convince me.

The world knows, that slavery as it existed among
the Romans, (which was the primary cause of their
destruction) was, comparatively speaking, no more
than a *cypher*, when compared with ours under the
Americans. Indeed I should not have noticed the
Roman slaves, had not the very learned and penetrating Mr. Jefferson said, "when a master was murdered, all his slaves in the same house, or within
hearing, were condemned to death."*—Here let me
ask Mr. Jefferson, (but he is gone to answer at the
bar of God, for the deeds done in his body while
living,) I therefore ask the whole American people,
had I not rather die, or be put to death, than to be
a slave to any tyrant, who takes not only my own,
but my wife and children's lives by the inches?
Yea, would I meet death with avidity far! far!!
in preference to such *servile submission* to the murderous hands of tyrants. Mr. Jefferson's very severe remarks on us have been so extensively argued
upon by men whose attainments in literature, I
shall never be able to reach, that I would not have
meddled with it, were it not to solicit each of my
brethren, who has the spirit of a man, to buy a copy
of Mr. Jefferson's " Notes on Virginia," and put it
in the hand of his son. For let no one of us suppose that the refutations which have been written
by our white friends are enough—they are *whites*—
we are *blacks*. We, and the world wish to see the

* See his Notes on Virginia, page 210.

3

charges of Mr. Jefferson refuted by the blacks
themselves, according to their chance; for we must
remember that what the whites have written respecting this subject, is other men's labours, and did
not emanate from the blacks.   I know well, that
there are some talents and learning among the coloured people of this country, which we have not a
chance to develope, in consequence of oppression;
but our oppression ought not to hinder us from ac-
quiring all we can.   For we will have a chance to
develope them by and by.   God will not suffer us,
always to be oppressed.   Our sufferings will come
to an *end*, in spite of all the Americans this side of
eternity.   Then we will want all the learning and
talents among ourselves, and perhaps more, to
govern ourselves.—" Every dog must have its day,"
the American's is coming to an end.

  But let us review Mr. Jefferson's remarks respecting us some further.   Comparing our miserable fathers, with the learned philosophers of Greece,
he says: "Yet notwithstanding these and other dis-
" couraging circumstances among the Romans, their
" slaves were often their rarest artists.   They ex-
" celled too, in science, insomuch as to be usually
"employed as tutors to their master's children;
"Epictetus, Terence and Phædrus, were slaves,—
" but they were of the race of whites.   It is not
" their *condition* then, but *nature*, which has pro-
" duced the distinction."*   See this, my brethren!!
Do you believe that this assertion is swallowed by
millions of the whites?   Do you know that Mr.
Jefferson was one of as great characters as ever lived
among the whites?   See his writings for the world,
and public labours for the United States of America.
Do you believe that the assertions of such a man,
will pass away into oblivion unobserved by this
people and the world?   If you do you are much mis-
taken—See how the American people treat us—
have we souls in our bodies?   Are we men who have

  * See his Notes on Virginia, page 211.

any spirits at all? I know that there are many *swell-bellied* fellows among us, whose greatest object is to fill their stomachs. Such I do not mean—I am after those who know and feel, that we are MEN, as well as other people ; to them, I say, that unless we try to refute Mr. Jefferson's arguments respecting us, we will only establish them.

But the slaves among the Romans. Every body who has read history, knows, that as soon as a slave among the Romans obtained his freedom, he could rise to the greatest eminence in the State, and there was no law instituted to hinder a slave from buying his freedom. Have not the Americans instituted laws to hinder us from obtaining our freedom? Do any deny this charge? Read the laws of Virginia, North Carolina, &c. Further: have not the Americans instituted laws to prohibit a man of colour from obtaining and holding any office whatever, under the government of the United States of America? Now, Mr. Jefferson tells us, that our condition is not so hard, as the slaves were under the Romans! ! ! ! ! !

It is time for me to bring this article to a close. But before I close it, I must observe to my brethren that at the close of the first Revolution in this country, with Great Britain, there were but thirteen States in the Union, now there are twenty-four, most of which are slave-holding States, and the whites are dragging us around in chains and in handcuffs, to their new States and Territories to work their mines and farms, to enrich them and their children—and millions of them believing firmly that we being a little darker than they, were made by our Creator to be an inheritance to them and their children for ever—the same as a parcel of *brutes*.

Are we MEN! !—I ask you, O my brethren! are we MEN? Did our Creator make us to be slaves to dust and ashes like ourselves? Are they not dying worms as well as we? Have they not to make their appearance before the tribunal of Heaven, to

answer for the deeds done in the body, as well as
we? Have we any other Master but Jesus Christ
alone? Is he not their Master as well as ours?—
What right then, have we to obey and call any other
Master, but Himself? How we could be so *submissive* to a gang of men, whom we cannot tell whether
they are *as good* as ourselves or not, I never could
conceive. However, this is shut up with the Lord,
and we cannot precisely tell—but I declare, we
judge men by their works.

The whites have always been an unjust, jealous,
unmerciful, avaricious and blood-thirsty set of beings, always seeking after power and authority.—
We view them all over the confederacy of Greece,
where they were first known to be any thing, (in
consequence of education) we see them there, cutting each other's throats—trying to subject each
other to wretchedness and misery—to effect which,
they used all kinds of deceitful, unfair, and unmerciful means. We view them next in Rome, where
the spirit of tyranny and deceit raged still higher.
We view them in Gaul, Spain, and in Britain.—
In fine, we view them all over Europe, together
with what were scattered about in Asia and Africa,
as heathens, and we see them acting more like devils
than accountable men. But some may ask, did not
the blacks of Africa, and the mulattoes of Asia, go
on in the same way as did the whites of Europe. I
answer, no—they never were half so avaricious, deceitful and unmerciful as the whites, according to
their knowledge.

But we will leave the whites or Europeans as
heathens, and take a view of them as Christians, in
which capacity we see them as cruel, if not more so
than ever. In fact, take them as a body, they are
ten times more cruel, avaricious and unmerciful than
ever they were; for while they were heathens, they
were bad enough it is true, but it is positively a fact
that they were not quite so audacious as to go and
take vessel loads of men, women and children, and

in cold blood, and through devilishness, throw them
into the sea, and murder them in all kind of ways.
While they were heathens, they were too ignorant
for such barbarity. But being Christians, enlightened and sensible, they are completely prepared
for such hellish cruelties. Now suppose God were
to give them more sense, what would they do? If
it were possible, would they not *dethrone* Jehovah
and seat themselves upon his throne? I therefore,
in the name and fear of the Lord God of Heaven
and of earth, divested of prejudice either on the
side of my colour or that of the whites, advance my
suspicion of them, whether they are *as good by nature* as we are or not. Their actions, since they
were known as a people, have been the reverse, I
do indeed suspect them, but this, as I before oberv-
ed, is shut up with the Lord, we cannot exactly
tell, it will be proved in succeeding generations.—
The whites have had the essence of the gospel as it
was preached by my master and his apostles—the
Ethiopians have not, who are to have it in its meridian splendor—the Lord will give it to them to
their satisfaction. I hope and pray my God, that
they will make good use of it, that it may be well
with them.*

---

* It is my solemn belief, that if ever the world becomes Chris-
tianized, (which must certainly take place before long) it will be
through the means, under God of the *Blacks*, who are now held in
wretchedness, and degradation, by the white *Christians* of the
world, who before they learn to do justice to us before our Maker—and be reconciled to us, and reconcile us to them, and by
that means have clear consciencies before God and man.—Send
out Missionaries to convert the Heathens, many of whom after
they cease to worship gods, which neither see nor hear, become
ten times more the children of Hell, then ever they were, why
what is the reason? Why the reason is obvious, they must learn
to do justice at home, before they go into distant lands, to dis-
play their charity, Christianity, and benevolence; when they learn
to do justice, God will accept their offering, (no man may think
that I am against Missionaries for I am not, my object is to see
justice done at home, before we go to convert the Heathens.)

ARTICLE II.

Ignorance, my brethren, is a mist, low down into
the very dark and almost impenetrable abyss in
which, our fathers for many centuries have been
plunged.   The Christians, and enlightened of Europe, and some of Asia, seeing the ignorance and
consequent degradation of our fathers, instead of
trying to enlighten them, by teaching them that religion and light with which God had blessed them,
they have plunged them into wretchedness ten thousand times more intolerable, than if they had left
them entirely to the Lord, and to add to their miseries, deep down into which they have plunged them
tell them, that they are an *inferior* and *distinct race*
of beings, which they will be glad enough to recal
and swallow by and by.   Fortune and misfortune,
two inseparable companions, lay rolled up in the
wheel of events, which have from the creation of
the world, and will continue to take place among
men until God shall dash worlds together.

When we take a retrospective view of the arts
and sciences—the wise legislators—the Pyramids,
and other magnificent buildings—the turning of the
channel of the river Nile, by the sons of Africa or
of Ham, among whom learning originated, and was
carried thence into Greece, where it was improved
upon and refined.   Thence among the Romans, and
all over the then enlightened parts of the world,
and it has been enlightening the dark and benighted
minds of men from then, down to this day.   I say,
when I view retrospectively, the renown of that
once mighty people, the children of our great pro-
genitor I am indeed cheered.   Yea further, when I
view that mighty son of Africa, HANNIBAL, one of
the greatest generals of antiquity, who defeated and

cut off so many thousands of the white Romans or murderers, and who carried his victorious arms, to the very gate of Rome, and I give it as my candid opinion, that had Carthage been well united and had given him good support, he would have carried that cruel and barbarous city by storm. But they were dis-united, as the coloured people are now, in the United States of America, the reason our natural enemies are enabled to keep their feet on our throats.

Beloved brethren—here let me tell you, and believe it, that the Lord our God, as true as he sits on his throne in heaven, and as true as our Saviour died to redeem the world, will give you a Hannibal, and when the Lord shall have raised him up, and given him to you for your possession, O my suffering brethren! remember the divisions and consequent sufferings of *Carthage* and of *Hayti*. Read the history particularly of Hayti, and see how they were butchered by the whites, and do you take warning. The person whom God shall give you, give him your support and let him go his length, and behold in him the salvation of your God. God will indeed, deliver you through him from your deplorable and wretched condition under the Christians of America. I charge you this day before my God to lay no obstacle in his way, but let him go.

The whites want slaves, and want us for their slaves, but some of them will curse the day they ever saw us. As true as the sun ever shone in its meridian splendor, my colour will root some of them out of the very face of the earth. They shall have enough of making slaves of, and butchering, and murdering us in the manner which they have. No doubt some may say that I write with a bad spirit, and that I being a black, wish these things to occur. Whether I write with a bad or a good spirit, I say if these things do not occur in their proper time, it is because the world in which we live does not exist, and we are deceived with regard to its existence.—

It is immaterial however to me, who believe, or who refuse—though I should like to see the whites repent peradventure God may have mercy on them, some however, have gone so far that their cup must be filled.

But what need have I to refer to antiquity, when Hayti, the glory of the blacks and terror of tyrants, is enough to convince the most avaricious and stupid of wretches—which is at this time, and I am sorry to say it, plagued with that scourge of nations, the Catholic religion; but I hope and pray God that she may yet rid herself of it, and adopt in its stead the Protestant faith; also, I hope that she may keep peace within her borders and be united, keeping a strict look out for tyrants, for if they get the least chance to injure her, they will avail themselves of it, as true as the Lord lives in heaven. But one thing which gives me joy is, that they are men who would be cut off to a man, before they would yield to the combined forces of the whole world—in fact, if the whole world was combined against them, it could not do any thing with them, unless the Lord delivers them up.

Ignorance and treachery one against the other—a grovelling servile and abject submission to the lash of tyrants, we see plainly, my brethren, are not the natural elements of the blacks, as the Americans try to make us believe; but these are misfortunes which God has suffered our fathers to be enveloped in for many ages, no doubt in consequence of their disobedience to their Maker, and which do, indeed, reign at this time among us, almost to the destruction of all other principles: for I must truly say, that ignorance, the mother of treachery and deceit, gnaws into our very vitals. Ignorance, as it now exits among us, produces a state of things, Oh my Lord! too horrible to present to the world. Any man who is curious to see the full force of ignorance developed among the coloured people of the United States of America, has only to go into the southern and western states of this confederacy, where, if he is not a tyrant, but has the feelings of a human being, who can feel for a fellow creature, he may see enough to make his very heart bleed! He may see there, a son take his mother, who bore almost the pains of death to give him birth, and by the command of a tyrant, strip her as naked as she came into the world, and apply the cow-hide to her, until she falls a victim to death in the road! He may see a husband take his dear wife, not unfrequently in a pregnant state, and perhaps far advanced, and beat her for an unmerciful wretch, until his infant falls a lifeless lump at her feet! Can the Americans escape God Almighty? If they do, can he be to us a God of Justice? God is just, and I know it—for he has convinced me to my satisfaction—I cannot doubt him. My observer may see fathers beating their sons, mothers their daughters, and children their parents, all to pacify the passions of unrelenting tyrants. He may also, see them telling news and lies, making mischief one upon another. These are some of the productions of ignorance, which he will see practised among my dear brethren, who are held in unjust slavery and wretchedness, by avaricious and unmerciful tyrants, to whom, and their hellish deeds, I would suffer my life to be taken before I would submit. And when my curious observer comes to take notice of those who are said to be free, (which assertion I deny) and who are making some frivolous pretentions to common sense, he will see that branch of ignorance among the slaves assuming a more cunning and deceitful course of procedure.— He may see some of my brethren in league with tyrants, selling their own brethren into *hell upon earth*, not dissimilar to the exhibitions in Africa, but in a more secret, servile and abject manner. Oh Heaven! I am full!!! I can hardly move my pen!!! and as I expect some will try to put me to death, to strike terror into others, and to obliterate from their minds the notion of freedom, so as to

4

keep my brethren the more secure in wretchedness, where they will be permitted to stay but a short time (whether tyrants believe it or not)—I shall give the world a development of facts, which are already witnessed in the courts of heaven. My observer may see some of those ignorant and treacherous creatures (coloured people) sneaking about in the large cities, endeavouring to find out all strange coloured people, where they work and where they reside, asking them questions, and trying to ascertain whether they are runaways or not, telling them, at the same time, that they always have been, are, and always will be, friends to their brethren ; and, perhaps, that they themselves are absconders, and a thousand such treacherous lies to get the better information of the more ignorant ! ! ! There have been and are at this day in Boston, New-York, Philadelphia, and Baltimore, coloured men, who are in league with tyrants, and who receive a great portion of their daily bread, of the moneys which they acquire from the blood and tears of their more miserable brethren, whom they scandalously delivered into the hands of our *natural enemies ! ! ! ! !*

To show the force of degraded ignorace and deceit among us some farther, I will give here an extract from a paragragh, which may be found in the Columbian Centinel of this city, for September 9, 1829, on the first page of which, the curious may find an article, headed

"AFFRAY AND MURDER."

" *Portsmouth, (Ohio) Aug.* 22, 1829.

" A most shocking outrage was committed in
" Kentucky, about eight miles from this place,
" on 14th inst. A negro driver, by the name of
" Gordon, who had purchased in Mayland about
" sixty negroes, was taking them, assisted by an
" associate named Allen, and the wagoner who con-
" veyed the baggage, to the Mississippi. The men
" were hand-cuffed and chained together, in the

" usual manner for driving those poor wretches,
" while the women and children were suffered to
" proceed without incumbrance. It appears that,
" by means of a file the negroes, unobserved, had suc-
" ceeded in separating the iron which bound their
" hands, in such a way as to be able to throw them
" off at any moment. About 8 o'clock in the morn-
" ing, while proceeding on the state road leading
" from Greenup to Vanceburg, two of them dropped
" their shackles and commenced a fight, when the
" wagoner (Petit) rushed in with his whip to com-
" pel them to desist. At this moment, every negro
" was found to be perfectly at liberty ; and one of
" them seizing a club, gave Petit a violent blow on
" the head, and laid him dead at his feet ; and Allen,
" who came to his assistance, met a similar fate,
" from the contents of a pistol fired by another of
" the gang. Gordon was then attacked, seized and
" held by one of the negroes, whilst another fired
" twice at him with a pistol, the ball of which each
" time grazed his head, but not proving effectual,
" he was beaten with clubs, and left for dead. They
" then commenced pillaging the wagon, and with an
" axe split open the trunk of Gordon, and rifled it
" of the money, about $2,400. Sixteen of the ne-
" groes then took to the woods ; Gordon, in the
" mean time, not being materially injured, was
" enabled, by the assistance of one of the women,
" to mount his horse and flee ; pursued, however,
" by one of the gang on another horse, with a drawn
" pistol ; fortunately he escaped with his life barely,
" arriving at a plantation, as the negro came in
" sight ; who then turned about and retreated.
    " The neighbourhood was immediately rallied,
" and a hot pursuit given—which, we understand,
" has resulted in the capture of the whole gang and
" the recovery of the greatest part of the money.
" Seven of the negro men and one woman, it is said
" were engaged in the murders, and will be brought
" to trial at the next court in Greenupsburg."

Here my brethren, I want you to notice particularly in the above article, the *ignorant* and *deceitful* *actions* of this coloured woman. I beg you to view it candidly, as for ETERNITY!!!! Here a *notorious* *wretch*, with two other confederates had SIXTY of them in a gang, driving them like *brutes*—the men all in chains and hand-cuffs, and by the help of God they got their chains and hand-cuffs thrown off, and caught two of the wretches and put them to death, and beat the other until they thought he was dead, and left him for dead; however, he deceived them, and rising from the ground, this *servile woman* helped him upon his horse, and he made his escape. Brethren, what do you think of this? Was it the natural *fine feelings* of this woman, to save such a wretch alive? I know that the blacks, take them half enlightened and ignorant, are more humane and merciful than the most enlightened and refined European that can be found in all the earth. Let no one say that I assert this because I am prejudiced on the side of my colour, and against the whites or Europeans. For what I write, I do it candidly, for my God and the good of both parties : Natural observations have taught me these things; there is a solemn awe in the hearts of the blacks, as it respects *murdering* men :* whereas the whites, (though they are great cowards) where they have the advantage, or think that there are any prospects of getting it, they murder all before them, in order to subject men to wretchedness and degradation under them. This is the natural result of pride and avarice. But I declare, the actions of this black woman are really insupportable. For my own part, I cannot think it was any thing but servile deceit, combined with the most gross ignorance : for we must remember that *humanity, kindness* and the *fear of the Lord*, does not consist in protecting *devils*. Here is a set of wretches, who had SIXTY of them in a gang, driving

---

* Which is the reason the whites take the advantage of us.

them around the country like *brutes*, to dig up gold and silver for them, (which they will get enough of yet.) Should the lives of such creatures be spared? Are God and Mammon in league? What has the Lord to do with a gang of desperate wretches, who go *sneaking about the country like robbers*—light upon his people wherever they can get a chance, binding them with chains and hand-cuffs, beat and murder them as they would *rattle-snakes?* Are they not the Lord's enemies? Ought they not to be destroyed? Any person who will save such wretches from destruction, is fighting against the Lord, and will receive his just recompense. The black men acted like *blockheads*. Why did they not make sure of the wretch? He would have made sure of them, if he could. It is just the way with black men—eight white men can frighten fifty of them; whereas, if you can only get courage into the blacks, I do declare it, that one good black man can put to death six white men; and I give it as a fact, let twelve black men get well armed for battle, and they will kill and put to flight fifty whites.— The reason is, the blacks, once you get them started, they glory in death. The whites have had us under them for more than three centuries, murdering, and treating us like brutes; and, as Mr. Jefferson wisely said, they have never *found us out*—they do not know, indeed, that there is an unconquerable disposition in the breasts of the blacks, which, when it is fully awakened and put in motion, will be subdued, only with the destruction of the animal existence. Get the blacks started, and if you do not have a gang of tigers and lions to deal with, I am a deceiver of the blacks and of the whites. How sixty of them could let that wretch escape unkilled, I cannot conceive—they will have to suffer as much for the two whom, they secured, as if they had put one hundred to death: if you commence, make sure work—do not trifle, for they will not trifle with you —they want us for their slaves, and think nothing

of murdering us in order to subject us to that wretched condition—therefore, if there is an *attempt* made
by us, kill or be killed. Now, I ask you, had you
not rather be killed than to be a slave to a tyrant,
who takes the life of your mother, wife, and dear
little children? Look upon your mother, wife and
children, and answer God Almighty; and believe
this, that it is no more harm for you to kill a man,
who is trying to kill you, than it is for you to take a
drink of water when thirsty; in fact, the man who
will stand still and let another murder him, is worse
than an infidel, and, if he has common sense, ought
not to be pitied. The actions of this deceitful and
ignorant coloured woman, in saving the life of a
desperate wretch, whose avaricious and cruel object
was to drive her, and her companions in miseries,
through the country like cattle, to make his fortune
on their carcasses, are but too much like that of
thousands of our brethren in these states: if any
thing is whispered by one, which has any allusion
to the melioration of their dreadful condition, they
run and tell tyrants, that they may be enabled to
keep them the longer in wretchedness and miseries.
Oh! coloured people of these United States, I ask
you, in the name of that God who made us, have
we, in consequence of oppression, nearly lost the
spirit of man, and, in no very trifling degree, adopt-
ed that of brutes? Do you answer, no?—I ask
you, then, what set of men can you point me to, in
all the world, who are so abjectly employed by
their oppressors, as we are by our *natural enemies*?
How can, Oh! how can those enemies but say that
we and our children are not of the HUMAN FAMILY,
but were made by our Creator to be an inheritance
to them and theirs for ever? How can the slave-
holders but say that they can bribe the best coloured person in the country, to sell his brethren for a
trifling sum of money, and take that atrocity to confirm them in their avaricious opinion, that we were
made to be slaves to them and their children? How

could Mr. Jefferson but say, *" I advance it there-
"fore as a suspicion only, that the blacks, whether
" originally a distinct race, or made distinct by
" time and circumstances, are *inferior* to the whites
" in the endowments both of body and mind?"—
" It," says he, " is not against experience to sup-
" pose, that different species of the same genius, or
" varieties of the same species, may possess differ-
" ent qualifications." [Here, my brethren, listen
to him.] ☞" Will not a lover of natural history,
" then, one who views the gradations in all the ra-
" ces of *animals* with the eye of philosophy, excuse
" an effort to keep those in the department of MAN
" as *distinct* as nature has formed them?"—I hope
" you will try to find out the meaning of this verse
—its widest sense and all its bearings : whether you
do or not, remember the whites do.   This very
verse, brethren, having emanated from Mr. Jefferson, a much greater philosopher the world never afforded, has in truth injured us more, and has been
as great a barrier to our emancipation as any thing
that has ever been advanced against us.   I hope
you will not let it pass unnoticed.   He goes on further, and says: " This *unfortunate* difference of
" colour, and *perhaps* of *faculty*, is a powerful obsta-
"cle to the emancipation of these people.   Many
" of their advocates, while they wish to vindicate the
" liberty of human nature are anxious also to pre-
" serve its *dignity* and *beauty*.   Some of these, em-
" barrassed by the question, 'What further is to be
" done with them?' join themselves in opposition
" with those who are actuated by sordid avarice
" only."   Now I ask you candidly, my suffering
brethren in time, who are candidates for the eternal
worlds, how could Mr. Jefferson but have given the
world these remarks respecting us, when we are so
submissive to them, and so much servile deceit pre-
vail among ourselves—when we so *meanly* submit

* See his Notes on Virginia, page 213.

to their murderous lashes, to which neither the Indians nor any other people under Heaven would
submit? No, they would die to a man, before they
would suffer such things from men who are no better than themselves, and *perhaps not so good.* Yes,
how can our friends but be embarrassed, as Mr.
Jefferson says, by the question, " What further is
to be done with these people ?" For while they are
working for our emancipation, we are, by our treachery, wickedness and deceit, working against ourselves and our children—helping ours, and the enemies of God, to keep us and our dear little children
in their infernal chains of slavery ! ! ! Indeed, our
friends cannot but relapse and join themselves
" with those who are actuated by *sordid avarice*
only ! ! ! !" For my own part, I am glad Mr. Jefferson has advanced his positions for your sake ; for
you will either have to contradict or confirm him
by your own actions, and not by what our friends
have said or done for us ; for those things are other
men's labours, and do not satisfy the Americans, who
are waiting for us to prove to them ourselves, that
we are MEN, before they will be willing to admit the
fact; for I pledge you my sacred word of honour,
that Mr. Jefferson's remarks respecting us, have
sunk deep into the hearts of millions of the whites,
and never will be removed this side of eternity.—
For how can they, when we are confirming him
every day, by our *groveling submissions* and *treachery?* I aver, that when I look over these United
States of America, and the world, and see the
ignorant deceptions and consequent wretchedness
of my brethren, I am brought oftimes solemnly to
a stand, and in the midst of my reflections I exclaim to my God, " Lord didst thou make us to be
slaves to our brethren, the whites?" But when I
reflect that God is just, and that millions of my
wretched brethren would meet death with glory—
yea, more, would plunge into the very mouths of
cannons and be torn into particles as minute as the

atoms which compose the elements of the earth, in preference to a mean submission to the lash of tyrants, I am with streaming eyes, compelled to shrink back into nothingness before my Maker, and exclaim again, thy will be done, O Lord God Almighty·

Men of colour, who are also of sense, for you particularly is my APPEAL designed. Our more ignorant brethren are not able to penetrate its value. I call upon you therefore to cast your eyes upon the wretchedness of your brethren, and to do your utmost to enlighten them—*go to work and enlighten your brethren!*—Let the Lord see you doing what you can to rescue them and yourselves from degradation. Do any of you say that you and your family are free and happy, and what have you to do with the wretched slaves and other people? So can I say, for I enjoy as much freedom as any of you, if I am not quite as well off as the best of you. Look into our freedom and happiness, and see of what kind they are composed!! They are of the very lowest kind—they are the very *dregs!*—they are the most servile and abject kind, that ever a people was in possession of! If any of you wish to know how FREE you are, let one of you start and go through the southern and western States of this country, and unless you travel as a slave to a white man (a servant is a *slave* to the man whom he serves) or have your free papers, (which if you are not careful they will get from you) if they do not take you up and put you in jail, and if you cannot give good evidence of your freedom, sell you into eternal slavery, I am not a living man : or any man of colour, immaterial who he is, or where he came from, if he is not *the fourth from the negro race!!* (as we are called) the white Christians of America will serve him the same they will sink him into wretchedness and degradation for ever while he lives. And yet some of you have the hardihood to say that you are free and happy! May God have mercy on your

5

freedom and happiness ! !   I met a coloured man
in the street a short time since, with a string of
boots on his shoulders; we fell into conversation,
and in course of which, I said to him, what a miserable set of people we are! He asked, why?—
Said I, we are so subjected under the whites, that
we cannot obtain the comforts of life, but by cleaning their boots and shoes, old clothes, waiting on
them, shaving them &c.   Said he, (with the boots
on his shoulders) " I am completely happy ! ! ! I
never want to live any better or happier than when
I can get a plenty of boots and shoes to clean ! ! !"
Oh ! how can those who are actuated by avarice
only, but think, that our Creator made us to be an
inheritance to them for ever, when they see that our
greatest glory is centered in such mean and low objects ? Understand me, brethren, I do not mean to
speak against the occupations by which we acquire
enough and sometimes scarcely that, to render ourselves and families comfortable through life.   I am
subjected to the same inconvenience, as you all.—
My objections are, to our *glorying* and being *happy*
in such low employments ; for if we are men, we
ought to be thankful to the Lord for the past, and
for the future.   Be looking forward with thankful
hearts to higher attainments than *wielding the razor*
and *cleaning boots and shoes.*   The man whose as-
pirations are not *above*, and even *below* these, is indeed, ignorant and wretched enough.   I advance it
therefore to you, not as a *problematical*, but as an unshaken and for ever immoveable *fact*, that your full
glory and happiness, as well as all other coloured
people under Heaven, shall never be fully consummated, but with the *entire emancipation of your en-
slaved brethren all over the world.*   You may therefore, go to work and do what you can to rescue, or
join in with tyrants to oppress them and yourselves,
until the Lord shall come upon you all like a thief
in the night.   For I believe it is the will of the Lord
that our greatest happiness shall consist in working

for the salvation of our whole body. When this is accomplished a burst of glory will shine upon you, which will indeed astonish you and the world. Do any of you say this never will be done? I assure you that God will accomplish it—if nothing else will answer, he will hurl tyrants and devils into *atoms* and make way for his people. But O my brethren! I say unto you again, you must go to work and prepare the way of the Lord.

There is a great work for you to do, as trifling as some of you may think of it. You have to prove to the Americans and the world, that we are MEN, and not *brutes*, as we have been represented, and by millions treated. Remember, to let the aim of your labours among your brethren, and particularly the youths, be the dissemination of education and religion.* It is lamentable, that many of our children go to school, from four until they are eight or ten, and sometimes fifteen years of age, and leave school knowing but a little more about the grammar of their language than a horse does about handling a musket—and not a few of them are really so ignorant, that they are unable to answer a person correctly, general questions in geography, and to hear them read, would only be to disgust a man who has a taste for reading; which, to do well, as trifling as it may appear to some, (to the ignorant in particular) is a great part of learning. Some few of them, may make out to scribble tolerably well, over a half sheet of paper, which I believe has hitherto been a powerful obstacle in our way, to keep us from ac-

---

* Never mind what the ignorant ones among us may say, many of whom when you speak to them for their good, and try to enlighten their minds, laugh at you, and perhaps tell you plump to your face, that they want no instruction from you or any other Niger, and all such aggravating language. Now if you are a man of understanding and sound sense, I conjure you in the name of the Lord, and of all that is good, to impute their actions to ignorance, and wink at their follies, and do your very best to get around them some way or other, for remember they are your brethren; and I declare to you that it is for your interests to teach and enlighten them.

quiring knowledge. An ignorant father, who knows
no more than what nature has taught him, together
with what little he acquires by the senses of hearing and seeing, finding his son able to write a neat
hand, sets it down for granted that he has as good
learning as any body ; the young, ignorant gump,
hearing his father or mother, who perhaps may be
ten times more ignorant, in point of literature, than
himself, extolling his learning, struts about, in the
full assurance, that his attainments in literature are
sufficient to take him through the world, when, in
fact, he has scarcely any learning at all ! ! ! !

I promiscuously fell in conversatson once, with
an elderly coloured man on the topics of education,
and of the great prevalency of ignorance among us :
Said he, " I know that our people are very ignorant
" but my son has a good education : I spent a great
" deal of money on his education : he can write as
" well as any white man, and I assure you that no
" one can fool him," &c. Said I, what else can your
son do, besides writing a good hand ? Can he post
a set of books in a mercantile manner ? Can he
write a neat piece of composition in prose or in
verse ? To these interogations he answered in the
negative. Said I, did your son learn, while he was
at school, the width and depth of English Grammar ?
To which he also replied in the negative, telling me
his son did not learn those things. Your son, said
I, then, has hardly any learning at all—he is almost
as ignorant, and more so, than many of those who
never went to school one day in all their lives. My
friend got a little put out, and so walking off, said
that his son could write as well as any white man.
Most of the coloured people, when they speak of the
education of one among us who can write a neat
hand, and who perhaps knows nothing but to scribble and puff pretty fair on a small scrap of paper,
immaterial whether his words are grammatical, or
spelt correctly, or not; if it only looks beautiful,
they say he has as good an education as any white

man—he can write as well as any white man, &c.
The poor, ignorant creature, hearing, this, he is
ashamed, forever after, to let any person see him
humbling himself to another for knowledge but going
about trying to deceive those who are more ignorant
than himself, he at last falls an ignorant victim to
death in wretchedness. I pray that the Lord may
undeceive my ignorant brethren, and permit them
to throw away pretensions, and seek after the substance of learning. I would crawl on my hands
and knees through mud and mire, to the feet of a
learned man, where I would sit and humbly suppli-
cate him to instil into me, that which neither devils
nor tyrants could remove, only with my life—for col-
ored people to acquire learning in this country, makes
tyrants quake and tremble on their sandy foundation. Why, what is the matter? Why, they know
that their infernal deeds of cruelty will be made
known to the world. Do you suppose one man of
good sense and learning would submit himself, his
father, mother, wife and children, to be slaves to a
wretched man like himself, who, instead of compensating him for his labours, chains, hand-cuffs and
beats him and family almost to death, leaving life
enough in them, however, to work for, and call him
master? No! no! he would cut his devilish throat
from ear to ear, and well do slave-holders know it.
The bare name of educating the coloured people,
scares our cruel oppressors almost to death. But if
they do not have enough to be frightened for yet, it
will be, because they can always keep us ignorant,
and because God approbates their cruelties, with
which they have been for centuries murdering us.
The whites shall have enough of the blacks, yet, as
true as God sits on his throne in Heaven.

Some of our brethren are so very full of learning,
that you cannot mention any thing to them which
they do not know better than yourself!!—nothing is
strange to them!!--they knew every thing years ago!
—if any thing should be mentioned in company

where they are, immaterial how important it is respecting us or the world, if they had not divulged
it; they make light of it, and affect to have known
it long before it was mentioned and try to make all
in the room, or wherever you may be, believe that
your conversation is nothing ! !—not worth hearing !
All this is the result of ignorance and ill-breeding;
for a man of good-breeding, sense and penetration,
if he had heard a subject told twenty times over, and
should happen to be in company where one should
commence telling it again, he would wait with pa-
tience on its narrator, and see if he would tell it as
it was told in his presence before—paying the most
strict attention to what is said, to see if any more
light will be thrown on the subject: for all men are
not gifted alike in telling, or even hearing the most
simple narration.   These ignorant, vicious, and
wretched men, contribute almost as much injury to
our body as tyrants themselves, by doing so much
for the promotion of ignorance amongst us; for
they, making such pretensions to knowledge, such
of our youth as are seeking after knowledge, and
can get access to them, take them as criterions to go
by, who will lead them into a channel, where, unless the Lord blesses them with the privilege of seeing their folly, they will be irretrievably lost forever, while in time ! ! !

    I must close this article by relating the very heart-
rending fact, that I have examined school-boys and
young men of colour in different parts of the country, in the most simple parts of Murray's English
Grammar, and not more than one in thirty was able
to give a correct answer to my interrogations.   If
any one contradicts me, let him step out of his door
into the streets of Boston, New-York, Philadelphia,
or Baltimore, (no use to mention any other, for the
Christians are too charitable further south or west !)
—I say, let him who disputes me, step out of his
door into the streets of either of those four cities,
and promiscuously collect one hundred school-boys,

or young men of colour, *who have been to school,*
and who are considered by the coloured people to
have received an excellent education, because, perhaps, some of them can write a good hand, but who,
notwithstanding their neat writing, may be almost
as ignorant, in comparison, as a horse.—And, I say
it, he will hardly find (in this enlightened day, and
in the midst of this *charitable* people) five in one
hundred, who, are able to correct the false grammar
of their language.—The cause of this almost universal ignorance among us, I appeal to our school-
masters to declare. Here is a fact, which I this
very minute take from the mouth of a young coloured man, who has been to school in this state
(Massachusetts) nearly nine years, and who knows
grammar this day, *nearly* as well as he did the day
he first entered the school-house, under a white
master. "This young man says : "My master
would never allow me to study grammar."   I asked him, why? "The school committee," said he
"forbid the coloured children learning grammar
" —they would not allow any but the white children
" to study grammar."   It is a notorious fact, that
the major part of the white Americans, have, ever
since we have been among them, tried to keep us
ignorant, and make us believe that God made us and
our children to be slaves to them and theirs.   *Oh !*
my God, have mercy on Christian Americans ! ! !

ARTICLE III.

OUR   WRETCHEDNESS   IN   CONSEQUENCE   OF   THE

PREACHERS OF THE RELIGION OF JESUS CHRIST.

Religion, my brethren, is a substance of deep
consideration among all nations of the earth.   The
Pagans have a kind, as well as the Mahometans,
the Jews and the Christians.   But pure and unde-
filed religion, such as was preached by Jesus Christ

and his apostles, is hard to be found in all the earth.
God, through his instrument, Moses, handed a dispensation of his Divine will, to the children of Israel
after they had left Egypt for the land of Canaan or
of Promise, who through hypocrisy, oppression and
unbelief, departed from the faith.—He then, by his
apostles, handed a dispensation of his, together with
the will of Jesus Christ, to the Europeans in Europe, who, in open violation of which, have made
merchandise of us, and it does appear as though
they take this very dispensation to aid them in their
infernal depredations upon us. Indeed, the way in
which religion was and is conducted by the Europeans and their descendants, one might believe it
was a plan fabricated by themselves and the *devils*
to oppress us. But hark! My master has taught
me better than to believe it—he has taught me that
his gospel as it was preached by himself and his
apostles remains the same, notwithstanding Europe
has tried to mingle blood and opression with it.

It is well known to the Christian world, that Bar-
tholomew Las Casas, that very very notoriously avaricious Catholic priest or preacher, and adventurer
with Columbus in his second voyage, proposed to
his countrymen, the Spaniards in Hispaniola to import the Africans from the Portuguese settlement
in Africa, to dig up gold and silver, and work their
plantations for them, to effect which, he made a
voyage thence to Spain, and opened the subject to
his master, Ferdinand then in declining health, who
listened to the plan: but who died soon after, and
left it in the hand of his successor, Charles V.*
This wretch, ("Las Casas, the Preacher,") suc-
ceeded so well in his plans of oppression, that in
1503, the first blacks had been imported into the
new world. Elated with this success, and stimulated
by sordid avarice only, he importuned Charles V. in

* See Butler's History of the United States, vol. 1, page 24.----
See also, page 25.

1511, to grant permission to a Flemish merchant, to import 4000 blacks at one time.* Thus we see, through the instrumentality of a pretended preacher of the gospel of Jesus Christ our common master, our wretchedness first commenced in America—where it has been continued from 1503, to this day, 1829. A period of three hundred and twenty-six years. But two hundred and nine, from 1620—when twenty of our fathers were brought into Jamestown, Virginia, by a Dutch man of war, and sold off like brutes to the highest bidders; and there is not a doubt in my mind, but that tyrants are in hope to perpetuate our miseries under them and their children until the final consumation of all things.—But if they do not get dreadfully deceived, it will be because God has forgotten them.

The Pagans, Jews and Mahometans try to make proselytes to their religions, and whatever human beings adopt their religions they extend to them their protection. But Christian Americans, not only hinder 'their fellow creatures, the Africans, but thousands of them *will absolutely beat a coloured person nearly to death, if they catch him on his knees, supplicating the throne of grace.* This barbarous cruelty was by all the heathen nations of antiquity, and is by the Pagans, Jews and Mahometans

---

* It is not unworthy of remark, that the Portuguese and Spaniards, were among, if not the very first Nations upon Earth, about three hundred and fifty or sixty years ago—But see what those *Christians* have come to now in consequence of afflicting our fathers and us, who have never molested, or disturbed them or any other of the white *Christians*, but have they received one quarter of what the Lord will yet bring upon them, for the murders they have inflicted upon us ?—They have had, and in some degree have now, sweet times on our blood and groans, the time however, of bitterness have sometime since commenced with them.—There is a God the Maker and preserver of all things, who will as sure as the world exists, give all his creatures their just recompense of reward in this and in the world to come,—we may fool or deceive, and keep each other in the most profound ignorance, beat murder and keep each other out of what is our lawful rights, or the rights of man, yet it is impossible for us to deceive or escape the Lord Almighty.

of the present day, left entirely to Christian Americans to inflict on the Africans and their descendants, that their cup which is nearly full may be completed. I have known tyrants or usurpers of human liberty in different parts of this country to take their fellow creatures, the coloured people, and beat them until they would scarcely leave life in them; what for? Why they say "The black devils had the audacity to be "found *making prayers and supplications to the* "*God who made them!!!!*" Yes, I have known small collections of coloured people to have convened together, for no other purpose than to worship God Almighty, in spirit and in truth, to the best of their knowledge; when tyrants, calling themselves *patrols*, would also convene and wait almost in breathless silence for the poor coloured people to commence singing and praying to the Lord our God, as soon as they had commenced, the wretches would burst in upon them and drag them out and commence beating them as they would rattle-snakes—many of whom, they would beat so unmercifully, that they would hardly be able to crawl for weeks and sometimes for months. Yet the American minister send out missionaries to convert the heathen, while they keep us and our children sunk at their feet in the most abject ignorance and wretchedness that ever a people was afflicted with since the world began. Will the Lord suffer this people to proceed much longer? Will he not stop them in their career? Does he regard the heathens abroad, more than the heathens among the Americans? Surely the Americans must believe that God is partial, notwithstanding his Apostle Peter, declared before Cornelius and others that he has no respect to persons, but in every nation he that feareth God and worketh righteousness is accepted with him.—"The word," said he, "which God "sent unto the children of Israel, preaching peace, "by Jesus Christ, (he is Lord of all."⁎) Have

---

⁎ See Acts of the Apostles, chap. x. v.—25—27.

not the Americans the Bible in their hands? Do
they believe it? Surely they do not. See how they
treat us in open violation of the Bible!! They no
doubt will be greatly offended with me, but if God
does not awaken them, it will be, because they are
superior to other men, as they have represented
themselves to be. Our divine Lord and Master said,
" all things whatsoever ye would that men should
" do unto you, do ye even so unto them." But an
American minister, with the Bible in is hand, holds
us and our children in the most abject slavery and
wretchedness. Now I ask them, would they like
for us to hold them and their children in abject
slavery and wretchedness? No says one, that never can be done—your are too abject and ignorant
to do it—you are not men—your were made to be
slaves to us, to dig up gold and silver for us and
our children. Know this, my dear sirs, that although
you treat us and our children now, as you do your
domestic beast—yet the final result of all future
events are known but to God Almighty alone, who
rules in the armies of heaven and among the inhabitants of the earth, and who dethrones one earthly
king and sits up another, as it seemeth good in his
holy sight. We may attribute these vicissitudes to
what we please, but the God of armies and of justice rules in heaven and in earth, and the whole
American people shall see and know it yet, to their
satisfaction. I have known pretended preachers of
the gospel of my Master, who not only held us as
their natural inheritance, but treated us with as
much rigor as any Infidel or Deist in the world—
just as though they were intent only on taking our
blood and groans to glorify the Lord Jesus Christ.
The wicked and ungodly, seeing their preachers
treat us with so much cruelty, they say : our preachers, who must be right, if any body are, treat them
like brutes, and why cannot we?—They think it is
no harm to keep them in slavery and put the whip
to them, and why cannot we do the same!—They

being preachers of the gospel of Jesus Christ, if it
were any harm, they would surely preach against
their oppression and do their utmost to erase it from
the country ; not only in one or two cities, but one
continual cry would be raised in all parts of this
confederacy, and would cease only with the complete overthrow of the system of slavery, in every
part of the country. But how far the American
preachers are from preaching against slavery and
oppression, which have carried their country to the
brink of a precipice; to save them from plunging
down the side of which, will hardly be affected, will
appear in the sequel of this paragraph, which I
shall narrate just as as it transpired.   I remember a
Camp Meeting in South Carolina, for which I em-
barked in a Steam Boat at Charleston, and having
been five or six hours on the water, we at last arriv-
ed at the place of hearing, where was a very great
concourse of people, who were no doubt, collected
together to hear the word of God, (that some had
collected barely as spectators to the scene, I will
not here pretend to doubt, however, that is left to
themselves and their God.)   Myself and boat companions, having been there a little while, we were
all called up to hear ; I among the rest went up
and took my seat—being seated, I fixed myself in a
complete position to hear the word of my Saviour
and to receive such as I thought was authenticated
by the Holy Scriptures; but to my no ordinary as-
tonishment, our Reverend gentleman got up and
told us (coloured people) that slaves must be obedient to their masters—must do their duty to their
masters or be whipped—the whip was made for the
backs of fools. &c.   Here I pause for a moment, to
give the world time to consider what was my sur-
prise, to hear such preaching from a minister of my
Master, whose very gospel is that of peace and not
of blood and whips, as this pretended preacher tried
to make us believe.   What the American preachers
can think of us, I aver this day before my God, I

have never been able to define. They have news-
papers and monthly periodicals, which they receive
in continual succession, but on the pages of which,
you will scarcely ever find a paragraph respecting
slavery, which is ten thousand times more injurious
to this country than all the other evils put together;
and which will be the final overthrow of its government, unless something is very speedily done; for
their cup is nearly full.—Perhaps they will laugh at
or make light of this; but I tell you Americans!
that unless you speedily alter your course, *you* and
your *Country are gone ! ! ! ! !* For God Almighty
will tear up the very face of the earth ! ! ! Will not
that very remarkable passage of Scripture be fulfill-
ed on Christian Americans? Hear it Americans ! !
" He that is unjust, let him be unjust still:—and he
" which is filthy, let him be filthy still: and he that
" is righteous, let him be righteous still: and he
" that is holy, let him be holy still."* I hope that
the Americans may hear, but I am afraid that they
have done us so much injury, and are so firm in the
belief that our Creator made us to be an inheritance
to them for ever, that their hearts will be hardened,
so that their destruction may be sure. This language, perhaps is too harsh for the American's delicate ears. But Oh Americans! Americans ! ! I
warn you in the name of the Lord, (whether you
will hear, or forbear,) to repent and reform, or you
are ruined ! ! ! Do you think that our blood is hid-
den from the Lord, because you can hide it from the
rest of the world, by sending out missionaries, and
by your charitable deeds to the Greeks, Irish, &c.?
Will he not publish your secret crimes on the house
top? Even here in Boston, pride and prejudice have
got to such a pitch, that in the very houses erected
to the Lord, they have built little places for the reception of coloured people, where they must sit dur-
ing meeting, or keep away from the house of God,

---

* See Revelation, chap. xxii. 11.

and the preachers say nothing about it—much less
go into the hedges and highways seeking the lost
sheep of the house of Israel, and try to bring them
in to their Lord and Master.   There are not a
more wretched, ignorant, miserable, and abject set
of beings in all the world, than the blacks in the
Southern and Western sections of this country, under tyrants and devils.   The preachers of America
cannot see them, but they can send out missionaries
to convert the heathens, notwithstanding.   Americans! unless you speedily alter your course of proceeding, if God Almighty does not stop you, I say
it in his name, that you may go on and do as you
please for ever, both in time and eternity—never
fear any evil at all ! ! ! ! ! ! ! !

    ☞ ADDITION.—The preachers and people of the
United States form societies against Free Masonry
and Intemperance, and write against Sabbath break-
ing, Sabbath mails, Infidelity, &c. &c.   But the
fountain head,* compared with which, all those
other evils are comparatively nothing, and from the
bloody and murderous head of which, they receive
no trifling support, is hardly noticed by the Americans.   This is a fair illustration of the state of society in this country—it shows what a bearing *avarice* has upon a people, when they are nearly given
up by the Lord to a hard heart and a reprobate
mind, in consequence of afflicting their fellow creatures.   God suffers some to go on until they are ruined for ever ! ! ! ! !   Will it be the case with
the whites of the United States of America?—
We hope not—we would not wish to see them
destroyed notwithstanding, they have and do now
treat us more cruel than any people have treated
another, on this earth since it came from the hands
of its Creator (with the exceptions of the French
and the Dutch, they treat us nearly as bad as the
Americans of the United States.)   The will of God
must however, in spite of us, *be done.*

---

* Slavery and oppression.

The English are the best friends the coloured people have upon earth. Though they have oppressed us a little and have colonies now in the West Indies, which oppress us *sorely.*—Yet notwithstanding they (the English) have done one hundred times more for the melioration of our condition, than all the other nations of the earth put together. The blacks cannot but respect the English as a nation, notwithstanding they have treated us a little cruel.

There is no intelligent *black man* who knows any thing, but esteems a real Englishman, let him see him in what part of the world he will—for they are the greatest benefactors we have upon earth. We have here and there, in other nations, good friends. But as a nation, the English are our friends.

How can the preachers and people of America believe the Bible? Does it teach them any distinction on account of a man's colour? Hearken, Americans! to the injunctions of our Lord and Master, to his humble followers.

* "And Jesus came and spake unto them, saying, "all power is given unto me in Heaven and in "earth.

"Go ye, therefore, and teach all nations, baptiz-"ing them in the name of the Father, and of the "Son, and of the Holy Ghost.

"Teaching them to observe all things whatsoever "I have commanded you; and lo, I am with you "alway, even unto the end of the world. Amen."

I declare, that the very face of these injunctions appear to be of God and not of man. They do not show the slightest degree of distinction. "Go ye "therefore," (says my divine Master) "and teach "all nations," (or in other words, all people) "bap-"tizing them in the name of the Father, and of the "Son, and of the Holy Ghost." Do you understand the above, Americans? We are a people, not-

* See St. Matthew's Gospel, chap. xxviii. 18, 19, 20. After Jesus was risen from the dead.

withstanding many of you doubt it. You have the
Bible in your hands, with this very injunction.—
Have you been to Africa, teaching the inhabitants
thereof the words of the Lord Jesus? "Baptizing
"them in the name of the Father, and of the Son,
"and of the Holy Ghost." Have you not, on the
contrary, entered among us, and learnt us the art of
throat-cutting, by setting us to fight, one against
another, to take each other as prisoners of war, and
sell to you for small bits of calicoes, old swords,
knives, &c. to make slaves for you and your children? This being done, have you not brought us
among you, in chains and hand-cuffs, like brutes,
and treated us with all the cruelties and rigour your
ingenuity could invent, consistent with the laws of
your country, which (for the blacks) are tyrannical
enough? Can the American preachers appeal unto
God, the Maker and Searcher of hearts, and tell
him, with the Bible in their hands, that they make
no distinction on account of men's colour? Can they
say, O God! thou knowest all things—thou knowest that we make no distinction between thy creatures, to whom we have to preach thy Word? Let
them answer the Lord; and if they cannot do it in
the affirmative, have they not departed from the
Lord Jesus Christ, their master? But some may
say, that they never had, or were in possession of a
religion, which made no distinction, and of course
they could not have departed from it. I ask you
then, in the name of the Lord, of what kind can
your religion be? Can it be that which was preached by our Lord Jesus Christ from Heaven? I believe you cannot be so wicked as to tell him that
his Gospel was that of *distinction*. What can the
American preachers and people take God to be?
Do they believe his words? If they do, do they believe that he will be mocked? Or do they believe,
because they are whites and we blacks, that God
will have respect to them? Did not God make us
all as it seemed best to himself? What right, then,

has one of us, to despise another, and to treat him
cruel, on account of his colour, which none, but the
God who made it can alter? Can there be a greater absurdity in nature, and particularly in a free republican country? But the Americans, having introduced slavery among them, their hearts have become almost seared, as with an hot iron, and God
has nearly given them up to believe a lie in preference to the truth ! ! ! And I am awfully afraid that
pride, prejudice, avarice and blood, will, before long
prove the final ruin of this happy republic, or land
of *liberty ! ! ! !* Can any thing be a greater mockery
of religion than the way in which it is conducted
by the Americans? It appears as though they are
bent only on daring God Almighty to do his best—
they chain and handcuff us and our children and
drive us around the country like brutes, and go into
the house of the God of justice to return him thanks
for having aided them in their infernal cruelties inflicted upon us. Will the Lord suffer this people
to go on much longer, taking his holy name in vain?
Will he not stop them, PREACHERS and all? O
Americans! Americans ! ! I call God—I call angels—I call men, to witness, that your DESTRUCTION
is at hand, and will be speedily consummated unless you RFPENT.

ARTICLE IV.

OUR WRETCHEDNESS IN CONSEQUENCE OF THE COLONIZING PLAN.

My dearly beloved brethren :—This is a scheme
on which so many able writers, together with that
very judicious coloured Baltimorean, have comment-
ed, that I feel my delicacy about touching it. But
as I am compelled to do the will of my Master, I
declare, I will give you my sentiments upon it.—
Previous, however, to giving my sentiments, either

7

for or against it, I shall give that of Mr. Henry Clay,
together with that of Mr. Elias B. Caldwell, Esq.
of the District of Columbia, as extracted from the
National Intelligencer, by Dr. Torrey, author of a
series of "Essays on Morals, and the Diffusion of
Useful Knowledge."

At a meeting which was convened in the District
of Columbia, for the express purpose of agitating
the subject of colonizing us in some part of the
world, Mr. Clay was called to the chair, and having
been seated a little while, he rose and spake, in
substance, as follows: says he—*"That class of the
"mixt population of our country [coloured people]
"was peculiarly situated ; they neither enjoyed the
"immunities of freemen, nor were they subjected
"to the incapacities of slaves, but partook, in some
"degree, of the qualities of both.   From their con-
"dition, and the unconquerable prejudices result-
"ing from their colour, they never could amalga-
"mate with the free whites of this country.   It was
"desirable, therefore, as it respected them, and the
"residue of the population of the country, to drain
"them off.   Various schemes of colonization had
"been thought of, and a part of our continent, it
"was supposed by some, might furnish a suitable
"establishment for them.   But, for his part, Mr. C.
"said, he had a decided preference for some part of
"the Coast of Africa.   There ample provision
"might be made for the colony itself, and it might
"be rendered instrumental to the introduction into
"that extensive quarter of the globe, of the arts,
"civilization, and Christianity."   [Here I ask Mr.
Clay, what kind of Christianity?   Did he mean
such as they have among the Americans—distinction, whip, blood and oppression?   I pray the Lord
Jesus Christ to forbid it.]   "There," said he, "was
"a peculiar, a moral fitness, in restoring them to the
"land of their fathers, and if instead of the evils and

---

* See Dr. Torrey's Portraiture of Domestic Slavery in the United States, page 85, 86.

" sufferings which we had been the innocent cause
" of inflicting upon the inhabitants of Africa, we
" can transmit to her the blessings of our arts, our
" civilization, and our religion. May we not hope
" that America will extinguish a great portion of
" that moral debt which she has contracted to that
" unfortunate continent? Can there be a nobler
" cause than that which, whilst it proposes, &c. * *
* * * * * [you know what this means.] "contem-
" plates the spreading of the arts of civilized life,
" and the possible redemption from ignorance and
" barbarism of a benighted quarter of the globe?"

Before I proceed any further, I solicit your notice, brethren, to the foregoing part of Mr. Clay's
speech, in which he says, (☞look above) "and if,
" instead of the evils and sufferings, which we had
" been the innocent cause of inflicting," &c.—
What this very learned statesman could have been
thinking about, when he said in his speech, "we had
" been the innocent cause of inflicting," &c., I have
never been able to conceive. Are Mr. Clay and
the rest of the Americans, innocent of the blood
and groans of our fathers and us, their children?—
Every individual may plead innocence, if he pleases,
but God will, before long, separate the innocent
from the guilty, unless someting is speedily done—
which I suppose will hardly be, so that their destruction may be sure. Oh Americans! let me tell
you, in the name of the Lord, it will be good for
you, if you listen to the voice of the Holy Ghost,
but if you do not, you are ruined ! ! ! Some of you
are good men; but the will of my God must be
done. Those avaricious and ungodly tyrants among
you, I am awfully afraid will drag down the vengeance of God upon you. When God Almighty
commences his battle on the continent of America,
for the oppression of his people, tyrants will wish
they never were born.

But to return to Mr. Clay, whence I digressed.
He says, "It was proper and necessary distinctly

" to state, that he understood it constituted no part
" of the object of this meeting, to touch or agitate
" in the slightest degree, a delicate question, con-
" nected with another portion of the coloured popu-
" lation of our country. It was not proposed to de-
" liberate upon or consider at all, any question of
" emancipation, or that which was connected with
" the abolition of slavery. It was upon that condi-
" tion alone, he was sure, that many gentlemen from
" the South and the West, whom he saw present,
" had attended, or could be expected to co-operate.
" It was upon that condition only, that he himself
" had attended."—That is to say, to fix a plan to get
those of the coloured people, who are said to be
free, away from among those of our brethren whom
they unjustly hold in bondage, so that they may be
enabled to keep them the more secure in ignorance
and wretchedness, to support them and their children, and consequently they would have the more
obedient slaves. For if the free are allowed to stay
among the slaves, they will have intercourse together, and, of course, the free will learn the slaves
bad habits, by teaching them that they are MEN,
as well as other people, and certainly *ought* and
must be FREE.

I presume, that every intelligent man of colour
must have some idea of Mr. Henry Clay, originally of Virginia, but now of Kentucky; they know
too, perhaps, whether he is a friend, or a foe to the
coloured citizens of this country, and of the world.
This gentleman, according to his own words, had
been highly favoured and blessed of the Lord,
though he did not acknowledge it; but, to the contrary, he acknowledged men, for all the blessings
with which God had favoured him. At a public
dinner, given him at Fowler's Garden, Lexington,
Kentucky, he delivered a public speech to a very
large concourse of people—in the concluding clause
of which, he says, "And now, my friends and fel-
" low citizens, I cannot part from you, on possi-

"bly the last occasion of my ever publicly addres-
"sing you, without reiterating the expression of
"my thanks, from a heart overflowing with grati-
"tude. I came among you, now more than thirty
"years ago, an orphan boy, pennyless, a stranger to
"you all, without friends, without the favour of the
"great, you took me up, cherished me, protected
"me, honoured me, you have constantly poured
"upon me a bold and unabated stream of innumer-
"able favours, time which wears out every thing
"has increased and strengthened your affection for
"me. When I seemed deserted by almost the
"whole world, and assailed by almost every tongue,
"and pen, and press, you have fearlessly and man-
"fully stood by me, with unsurpassed zeal and un-
"diminished friendship. When I felt as if I should
"sink beneath the storm of abuse and detraction,
"which was violently raging around me, I have
"found myself upheld and sustained by your en-
"couraging voices and approving smiles. I have
"doubtless, committed many faults and indiscre-
"tions, over which you have thrown the broad man-
"tle of your charity. But I can say, and in the
"presence of God and in this assembled multitude, I
"will say, that I have honestly and faithfully serv-
"ed my country—that I have never wronged it—
"and that, however unprepared, I lament that I am
"to appear in the Divine presence on other ac-
"counts, I invoke the stern justice of his judgment
"on my public conduct, without the slightest ap-
"prehension of his displeasure."

Hearken to this Statesman indeed, but no philanthropist, whom God sent into Kentucky, an orphan
boy, pennyless, and friendless, where he not only
gave him a plenty of friends and the comforts of life,
but raised him almost to the very highest honour in
the nation, where his great talents, with which the
Lord has been pleased to bless him, has gained for
him the affection of a great portion of the people
with whom he had to do. But what has this gen-

tleman done for the Lord, after having done so much
for him ?   The Lord has a suffering people, whose
moans and groans at his feet for deliverance from
oppression and wretchedness, pierce the very throne
of Heaven, and call loudly on the God of Justice,
to be revenged.   Now, what this gentleman, who
is so highly favoured of the Lord, has done to liberate those miserable victims of oppression, shall
appear before the world, by his letters to Mr. Gallatin, Envoy Extraordinary and Minister Plenipo-
tentiary to Great Britain, dated June 19, 1826.—
Though Mr. Clay was writing for the States, yet
nevertheless, it appears, from the very face of his
letters to that gentleman, that he was as anxious, if
not more so, to get those free people and sink them
into wretchedness, as his constituents, for whom he
wrote.

The Americans of North and of South America,
including the West India Islands—no trifling portion of whom were, for stealing, murdering, &c.
compelled to flee from Europe, to save their necks
or banishment, have effected their escape to this
continent, where God blessed them with all the
comforts of life—He gave them a plenty of every
thing calculated to do them good—not satisfied with
this, however, they wanted slaves, and wanted us
for their slaves, who belong to the Holy Ghost, and
no other, who we shall have to serve instead of tyrants.—I say, the Americans want us, the property
of the Holy Ghost, to serve them.   But there is a
day fast approaching, when (unless there is a universal repentance on the part of the whites, which
will scarcely take place, they have got to be so hardened in consequence of our blood, and so wise in
their own conceit.)   To be plain and candid with
you, Americans !   I say that the day is fast approaching, when there will be a greater time on the continent of America, than ever was witnessed upon this
earth,since it came from the hand of its Creator. Some
of you have done us so much injury,that you will nev-

er be able to repent.—Your cup must be filled.—You
want us for your slaves, and shall have enough of us
—God is just, *who will give you your fill of us.* But
Mr. Henry Clay, speaking to Mr. Gallatin, respecting coloured people, who had effected their escape
from the U. States (or to them *hell upon earth ! ! !*)
to the hospitable shores of Canada,* from whence it
would cause more than the lives of the Americans to
get them, to plunge into wretchedness—he says:
" The General Assembly of Kentucky, one of the
" states which is most affected by the escape of slaves
" into Upper Canada, has again, at their session
" which has just terminated, invoked the interposi-
" tion of the General Government. In the treaty
" which has been recently concluded with the Uni-
" ted Mexican States, and which is now under the
" consideration of the Senate, provision is made for
" the restoration of fugitive slaves. As it appears
" from your statements of what passed on that sub-
" ject, with the British Plenipotentiaries, that they
" admitted the correctness of the principle of resto-
" ration, it is hoped that you will be able to suc-
" ceed in making satisfactory arrangements."
   There are a series of these letters, all of which are
to the same amount; some however, presenting a
face more of his own responsibility. I wonder what
would this gentleman think, if the Lord should give
him among the rest of his blessings enough of slaves?
Could he blame any other being but himself? Do
we not belong to the Holy Ghost? What business
has he or any body else, to be sending letters about
the world respecting us? Can we not go where we
want to, as well as other people, only if we obey the
voice of the Holy Ghost? This gentleman, (Mr. Henry Clay) not only took an active part in this colonizing plan, but was absolutely chairman of a meeting
held at Washington, the 21st day of December 1816,†

* Among the English, our real friends and benefactors.

† In the first edition of this work, it should read 1816, as above,
and not 1826, as it there appears.

to agitate the subject of colonizing us in Africa.—
Now I appeal and ask every citizen of these United
States and of the world, both *white* and *black*, who
has any knowledge of Mr. Clay's public labor for
these States—I want you candidly to answer the
Lord, who sees the secrets of our hearts.—Do you
believe that Mr. Henry Clay, late Secretary of State,
and now in Kentucky, is a friend to the blacks, further, than his personal interest extends? Is it not
his greatest object and glory upon earth, to sink us
into miseries and wretchedness by making slaves of
us, to work his plantation to enrich him and his family? Does he care a pinch of snuff about Africa—
whether it remains a land of Pagans and of blood, or
of Christians, so long as he gets enough of her sons
and daughters to dig up gold and silver for him? If
he had no slaves, and could obtain them in no other
way if it were not, repugnant to the laws of his country, which prohibit the importation of slaves (which
act was, indeed, more through apprehension than
humanity) would he not try to import a few from
Africa, to work his farm? Would he work in the hot
sun to earn his bread, if he could make an African work for nothing, particularly, if he could keep
him in ignorance and make him believe that God
made him for nothing else but to work for him? Is
not Mr. Clay a white man, and too delicate to work
in the hot sun!! Was he not made by his Creator to
sit in the shade, and make the blacks work without
remuneration for their services, to support him and
his family!!! I have been for some time taking notice
of this man's speeches and public writings, but never
to my knowledge have I seen any thing in his writings which insisted on the emancipation of slavery,
which has almost ruined his country. Thus we see
the depravity of men's hearts, when in pursuit only of
gain—particularly when they oppress their fellow
creatures to obtain that gain—God suffers some to
go on until they are lost forever. This same Mr.
Clay, wants to know, what he has done, to merit the

disapprobation of the American people. In a public speech delivered by him, he asked: "Did I in-
"volve my country in an unnecessary war?" to merit the censure of the Americans—"Did I bring
"obliquy upon the nation, or the people whom I
"represented?—did I ever lose any opportunity to
"advance the fame, honor and prosperity of this
"State and the Union?" How astonishing it is,
for a man who knows so much about God and his
ways, as Mr. Clay, to ask such frivolous questions?
Does he believe that a man of his talents and standing in the midst of a people, will get along unnoticed
by the penetrating and all seeing eye of God, who is
continually taking cognizance of the hearts of men?
Is not God against him, for advocating the murderous cause of slavery? If God is against him, what
can the Americans, together with the whole world
do for him? Can they save him from the hand of
the Lord Jesus Christ?

I shall now pass in review the speech of Mr. Elias B. Caldwell, Esq. of the District of Columbia,
extracted from the same page on which Mr. Clay's
will be found. Mr. Caldwell, giving his opinion
respecting us, at that ever memorable meeting, he
says: "The more you improve the condition of
"these people, the more you cultivate their minds,
"the more miserable you make them in their pre-
"sent state. You give them a higher relish for
"those privileges which they can never attain, and
"turn what we intend for a blessing into a curse."
Let me ask this benevolent man, what he means by
a blessing intended for us? Did he mean sinking
us and our children into ignorance and wretchedness, to support him and his family? What he
meant will appear evident and obvious to the most
ignorant in the world ☞ See Mr. Caldwell's intended blessings for us, O! my Lord!! "No,"
said he, "if they must remain in their present situa-
"tion, keep them in the *lowest state of degradation*
"*and ignorance.* The nearer you bring them to

8

" the condition of brutes, the better chance do you
" give them of possessing their *apathy*."   Here I
pause to get breath, having labored to extract the
above clause of this gentleman's speech, at that colonizing meeting.   I presume that every body knows
the meaning of the word " *apathy*,"—if any do not,
let him get Sheridan's Dictionary, in which he will
find it explained in full.   I solicit the attention of
the world, to the foregoing part of Mr. Caldwell's
speech, that they may see what man will do with
his fellow men, when he has them under his feet.
To what length will not man go in iniquity when
given up to a hard heart, and reprobate mind, in
consequence of blood and oppression ?   The last
clause of this speech, which was written in a very
artful manner, and which will be taken for the speech
of a friend, without close examination and deep
penetration, I shall now present. He says, " surely,
" Americans ought to be the last people on earth,
" to advocate such slavish doctrines, to cry peace
" and contentment to those who are deprived of the
" privileges of civil liberty, they who have so large-
" ly partaken of its blessings, who know so well
" how to estimate its value, ought to be among the
" foremost to extend it to others."   The real sense
and meaning of the last part of Mr. Caldwell's speech
is, get the free people of colour away to Africa,
from among the slaves, where they may at once be
blessed and happy, and those who we hold in slavery, will be contented to rest in ignorance and
wretchedness, to dig up gold and silver for us and
our children.   Men have indeed got to be so cunning, these days, that it would take the eye of a
Solomon to penetrate and find them out.

    Addition.—Our dear Redeemer said, "There-
" fore, whatsoever ye have spoken in darkness, shall
" be heard in the light; and that which ye have
" spoken in the ear in closets, shall be proclaimed
" upon the house tops."

    How obviously this declaration of our Lord

has been shown among the Americans of the United States. They have hitherto passed among some nations, who do not know any thing about their internal concerns, for the most enlightened, humane, charitable, and merciful people upon earth, when at the same time they treat us, the (coloured people) secretly more cruel and unmerciful than any other nation upon earth.—It is a fact, that in our Southern and Western States, there are millions who hold us in chains or in slavery, whose greatest object and glory, is centered in keeping us sunk in the most profound ignorance and stupidity, to make us work without remunerations for our services. Many of whom if they catch a coloured person, whom they hold in unjust ignorance, slavery and degradation, to them and their children, with a book in his hand, will beat him nearly to death. I heard a wretch in the state of North Carolina said, that if any man would teach a black person whom he held in slavery, to spell, read or write, he would prosecute him to the very extent of the law.— Said the ignorant wretch,* "a Nigar, ought not to have any more sense than enough to work for his master." May I not ask to fatten the wretch and his family ?—These and similar cruelties these *Christians* have been for hundreds of years inflicting on our fathers and us in the dark, God has however, very recently published some of their secret crimes on the house top, that the world may gaze on their Christianity and see of what kind it is composed.—Georgia for instance, God has completely shown to the world, the *Christianity* among its white *inhabitants.* A law has recently passed the Legislature of this *republican* State (Georgia) prohibiting all free or slave persons of colour, from learning to read or write ; another law has passed the *re-*

---

* It is a fact, that in all our Slave-holding States (in the countries) there are thousands of the whites, who are almost as ignorant in comparison as horses, the most they know, is to beat the coloured people, which some of them shall have their hearts full of yet.

publican House of Delegates, (but not the Senate) in Virginia, to prohibit all persons of colour, (free and slave) from learning to read or write, and even to hinder them from meeting together in order to worship our Maker !!!!!!—Now I solemnly appeal, to the most skilful historians in the world, and all those who are mostly acquainted with the histories of the Antideluvians and of Sodom and Gomorrah, to show me a parallel of barbarity. *Christians ! ! Christians ! ! !* I dare you to show me a parallel of cruelties in the annals of Heathens or of Devils, with those of Ohio, Virginia and of Georgia—know the world that these things were before done in the dark, or in a corner under a garb of humanity and religion. God has however, taken of the fig-leaf covering, and made them expose themselves on the house top. I tell you that God works in many ways his wonders to perform, he will unless they repent, make them expose themselves enough more yet to the world.—See the acts of the *Christians* in FLORIDA, SOUTH CAROLINA, and KEN-TUCKY—was it not for the reputation of the house of my Lord and Master, I would mention here, an act of cruelty inflicted a few days since on a black man, by the white *Christians* in the PARK STREET CHURCH, in this (CITY) which is almost enough to make Demons themselves quake and tremble in their FIREY HABITATIONS.— Oh ! my Lord how refined in iniquity the whites have got to be in consequence of our blood*—what kind !! Oh ! what kind !!! of Christianity can be found this day in all the earth ! ! ! ! ! !

I write without the fear of man, I am writing for my God, and fear none but himself; they may put me to death if they choose—(I fear and esteem a

---

* The Blood of our fathers who have been murdered by the whites, and the groans of our Brethren, who are now held in cruel ignorance, wretchedness and slavery by them, cry aloud to the Maker of Heaven and of earth, against the whole continent of America, for redresses.

good man however, let him be black or white.) I
forbear to comment on the cruelties inflicted on this
Black Man by the Whites, in the Park Street
Meeting House, I will leave it in the dark!!!!!
But I declare that the atrocity is really to Heaven
daring and infernal, that I must say that God has
commenced a course of exposition among the Americans, and the glorious and heavenly work will continue to progress until they learn to do justice.

Extract from the Speech of Mr. John Randolph,
of Roanoke.

Said he :—" It had been properly observed by the
" Chairman, as well as by the gentleman from this
" District (meaning Messrs. Clay and Caldwell) that
" there was nothing in the proposition submitted to
" consideration which in the smallest degree touches
" another very important and delicate question,
" which ought to be left as much out of view as possi-
" ble, (Negro Slavery.)*

" There is no fear, Mr. R. said that this proposi-
" tion would alarm the slave-holders ; they had been
" accustomed to think seriously of the subject.—
" There was a popular work on agriculture, by John
" Taylor of Carolina, which was widely circulated,
" and much confided in, in Virginia. In that book,
" much read because coming from a practical man,
" this description of people, [referring to us half
" free ones] were pointed out as a great evil. They
" had indeed been held up as the greater bug-bear
" to every man who feels an inclination to eman-
" cipate his slaves, not to create in the bosom
" of his country so great a nuisance. If a place
" could be provided for their reception, and a

---

* " Niger," is a word derived from the Latin, which was used by
the old Romans, to designate inanimate beings, which were black :
such as soot, pot, wood, house, &c. Also, animals which they
considered inferior to the human species, as a black horse, cow,
hog, bird, dog, &c. The white Americans have applied this term
to Africans, by way of reproach for our colour, to aggravate and
heighten our miseries, because they have their feet on our throats.

"" mode of sending them hence, there were hun-
" dreds, nay thousands of citizens who would, by
" manumitting their slaves, relieve themselves from
" the cares attendant on their possession. The
" great slave-holder, Mr. R. said, was frequently a
" mere sentry at his own door—bound to stay on
" his plantation to see that his slaves were properly
" treated, &c. Mr. R. concluded by saying, that
" he had thought it necessary to make these remarks
" being a slave-holder himself, to shew that, so far
" from being connected with abolition of slavery,
" the measure proposed would prove one of the great-
" est securities to enable the master to keep in pos-
" session his own property."

Here is a demonstrative proof, of a plan got up,
by a gang of slave-holders to select the free people
of colour from among the slaves, that our more miserable brethren may be the better secured in ignorance and wretchedness, to work their farms and
dig their mines, and thus go on enriching the
Christians with their blood and groans. What our
brethren could have been thinking ubout, who have
left their native land and home and gone away to
Africa, I am unable to say. This country is as much
ours as it is the whites, whether they will admit it
now or not, they will see and believe it by and by.
They tell us about prejudice—what have we to do
with it? Their prejudices will be obliged to fall
like lightning to the ground, in succeeding generations; not, however, with the will and consent of
all the whites, for some will be obliged to hold on
to the old adage, viz: the blacks are not men, but
were made to be an inheritance to us and our children for ever ! ! ! ! ! ! I hope the residue of the coloured people, will stand still and see the salvation
of God and the miracle which he will work for
our delivery from wretchedness under the Christians ! ! ! ! ! !

☞ ADDITION.—If any of us see fit to go away,
go to those who have been for many years, and are

now our greatest earthly friends and benefactors—
the English. If not so, go to our brethren, the Hay-
tians, who, according to their word, are bound to protect and comfort us. The Americans say, that we
are ungrateful—but I ask them for heaven's sake,
what should we be grateful to them for—for murdering our fathers and mothers?—Or do they wish
us to return thanks to them for chaining and hand-
cuffing us, branding us, cramming fire down our
throats, or for keeping us in slavery, and beating us
nearly or quite to death to make us work in ignorance and miseries, to support them and their families. They certainly think that we are a gang of
fools. Those among them, who have volunteered
their services for our redemption, though we are
unable to compensate them for their labours, we
nevertheless thank them from the bottom of our
hearts, and have our eyes steadfastly fixed upon
them, and their labours of love for God and man.—
But do slave-holders think that we thank them for
keeping us in miseries, and taking our lives by the
inches?

Before I proceed further with this scheme, I shall
give an extract from the letter of that truly Reverend Divine, (Bishop Allen,) of Philadelphia, respecting this trick. At the instance of the editor
of the Freedom's Journal, he says, * " Dear Sir, I
have been for several years trying to reconcile my
mind to the Colonizing of Africans in Liberia, but
there have always been, and there still remain great
and insurmountable objections against the scheme.
We are an unlettered people, brought up in ignorance, not one in a hundred can read or write, not
one in a thousand has a liberal education; is there
any fitness for such to be sent into a far country,
among heathens, to convert or civilize them, when
they themselves are neither civilized or Christian-
ized? See the great bulk of the poor, ignorant Africans in this country, exposed to every temptation

* See Freedom's Journal for Nov. 2d, 1827—vol. 1, No. 34.

before them : all for the want of their morals being
refined by education and proper attendance paid
unto them by their owners, or those who had the
charge of them. It is said by the Southern slave-
holders, that the more ignorant they can bring up
the Africans, the better slaves they make, ('go and
come.') Is there any fitness for such people to be colonized in a far country to be their own rulers? Can
we not discern the project of sending the free people of colour away from their country? Is it not for
the interest of the slave-holders to select the free
people of colour out of the different states, and send
them to Liberia? Will it not make their slaves un-
easy to see free men of colour enjoying liberty? It
is against the law in some of the Southern States,
that a person of colour should receive an education,
under a severe penalty. Colonizationists speak of
America being first colonized; but is there any
comparison between the two? America was colonized by as *wise, judicious* and *educated* men as the
world afforded. WILLIAM PENN did not want for
learning, wisdom, or *intelligence.* If all the people
in Europe and America were as ignorant and in the
same situation as our brethren, what would become
of the world? Where would be the principle or
piety that would govern the people? We were
stolen from our mother country, and brought *here.*
We have *tilled* the ground and made fortunes for
thousands, and still they are not weary of our services. *But they who stay to till the ground must be
slaves.* Is there not land enough in America, or
' corn enough in Egypt?' Why should they send
us into a far country to die? See the thousands of
foreigners emigrating to America every year : and
if there be ground sufficient for them to cultivate,
and bread for them to eat, why would they wish to
send the *first tillers* of the land away? Africans
have made fortunes for thousands, who are yet unwilling to part with their services; but the free
must be sent away, and those who remain, must be

slaves. I have no doubt that there are many good men who do not see as I do, and who are for sending us to Liberia; but they have not duly considered the subject—they are not men of colour.— This land which we have watered with our *tears* and *our blood*, is now our *mother country*, and we are well satisfied to stay where wisdom abounds and the gospel is free."

"RICHARD ALLEN,
" *Bishop of the African Methodist Episcopal*
" *Church in the United States.*"

I have given you, my brethren, an extract verbatim, from the letter of that godly man, as you may find it on the aforementioned page of Freedom's Journal. I know that thousands, and perhaps millions of my brethren in these States, have never heard of such a man as Bishop Allen— a man whom God many years ago raised up among his ignorant and degraded brethren, to preach Jesus Christ and him crucified to them—who notwithstanding, had to wrestle against principalities and the powers of darkness to diffuse that gospel with which he was endowed among his brethren—but who having overcome the combined powers of devils and wicked men, has under God planted a Church among us which will be as durable as the foundation of the earth on which it stands. Richard Allen! O my God!! The bare recollection of the labours of this man, and his ministers among his deplorably wretched brethren, (rendered so by the whites) to bring them to a knowledge of the God of Heaven, fills my soul with all those very high emotions which would take the pen of an Addison to portray. It is impossible my brethren for me to say much in this work respecting that man of God. When the Lord shall raise up coloured historians in succeeding generations, to present the crimes of this nation, to the then gazing world, the Holy Ghost will make them do justice to the name of Bishop Allen, of Philadel-

9

phia.   Suffice it for me to say, that the name of this
very man (Richard Allen) though now in obscuri-
ty and degradation, will notwithstanding, stand on
the pages of history among the greatest divines who
have lived since the apostolic age, and among the
Africans, Bishop Allen's will be entirely pre-emi-
nent.   My brethren, search after the character and
exploits of this godly man among his ignorant and
miserable brethren, to bring them to a knowledge
of the truth as it is in our Master.   Consider upon
the tyrants and false Christians against whom he
had to contend in order to get access to his brethren.   See him and his ministers in the States of
New York, New Jersey, Pennsylvania, Delaware
and Maryland, carrying the gladsome tidings of free
and full salvation to the coloured people.   Tyrants
and false Christians however, would not allow him to
penetrate far into the South, for fear that he would
awaken some of his ignorant brethren, whom they
held in wretchedness and misery—for fear, I say it,
that he would awaken and bring them to a knowledge of their Maker.   O my Master! my Master!
I cannot but think upon Christian Americans!!!—
What kind of people can they be?   Will not those
who were burnt up in Sodom and Gomorrah rise
up in judgment against Christian Americans with
the Bible in their hands, and condemn them?   Will
not the Scribes and Pharisees of Jerusalem, who
had nothing but the laws of Moses and the Prophets
to go by, rise up in judgment against Christian
Americans, and condemn them,* who, in addition to
these have a revelation from Jesus Christ the Son
of the living God?   In fine, will not the Antideluvians, together with the whole heathen world of antiquity, rise up in judgment against Christian Americans and condemn them?   The Christians of Europe and America go to Africa, bring us away, and

---

* I mean those whose labours for the good, or rather destruction
of Jerusalem, and the Jews.   Ceased before our Lord entered the
Temple, and overturned the tables of the Money Changers.

throw us into the seas, and in other ways murder
us, as they would wild beast.   The Antideluvians
and heathens never dreamed of such barbarities.—
Now the Christians believe, because they have a
name to live, while they are dead, that God will
overlook such things.   But if he does not deceive
them, it will be because he has overlooked it sure
enough.   But to return to this godly man, Bishop
Allen.   I do hereby openly affirm it to the world,
that he has done more in a spiritual sense for his ignorant and wretched brethren than any other man
of colour has, since the world began.   And as for
the greater part of the whites, it has hitherto been
their greatest object and glory to keep us ignorant
of our Maker, so as to make us believe that we were
made to be slaves to them and their children, to dig
up gold and silver for them.   It is notorious that
not a few professing Christians among the whites,
who profess to love our Lord and Saviour Jesus
Christ, have assailed this man and laid all the obsta-
cles in his way they possibly could, consistent with
their profession—and what for?   Why, their course
of proceeding and his, clashed exactly together—
they trying their best to keep us ignorant, that we
might be the better and more obedient slaves—
while he, on the other hand, doing his very best to
enlighten us and teach us a knowledge of the Lord.
And I am sorry that I have it to say, that many of
our brethren have joined in with our oppressors,
whose dearest objects are only to keep us ignorant
and miserable against this man to stay his hand.—
However, they have kept us in so much ignorance,
that many of us know no better than to fight against
ourselves, and by that means strengthen the hands
of our natural enemies, to rivet their infernal chains
of slavery upon us and our children.   I have several times called the white Americans our *natural enemies*—I shall here define my meaning of the phrase.
Shem, Ham and Japheth, together with their father
Noah and wives, I believe were not natural ene-

mies to each other. When the ark rested after the
flood upon Mount Arrarat, in Asia, they (eight)
were all the people which could be found alive in
all the earth—in fact if Scriptures be true, (which
I believe are) there were no other living men in
all the earth, notwithstanding some ignorant creatures hesitate not to tell us that we, (the blacks) are
the seed of Cain the murderer of his brother Abel.
But where or of whom those ignorant and avaricious
wretches could have got their information, I am unable to declare. Did they receive it from the Bible? I have searched the Bible as well as they, if
I am not as well learned as they are, and have never
seen a verse which testifies whether we are the seed
of Cain or of Abel. Yet those men tell us that we
are the seed of Cain, and that God put a dark stain
upon us, that we might be known as their slaves!!!
Now, I ask those avaricious and ignorant wretches,
who act more like the seed of Cain, by murdering
the whites or the blacks? How many vessel loads
of human beings, have the blacks thrown into the
seas? How many thousand souls have the blacks
murdered in cold blood, to make them work in
wretchedness and ignorance, to support them and
their families?*—However, let us be the seed of
Cain, Harry, Dick, or *Tom*!!! God will show the
whites what we are, yet. I say, from the beginning, I do not think that we were natural enemies
to each other. But the whites having made us so
wretched, by subjecting us to slavery, and having
murdered so many millions of us, in order to make
us work for them, and out of devilishness—and
they taking our wives, whom we love as we do
ourselves—-our mothers, who bore the pains of
death to give us birth—our fathers and dear lit-

---

* How many millions souls of the human family have the blacks
beat nearly to death, to keep them from learning to read the Word
of God, and from writing. And telling lies about them, by holding
them up to the world as a tribe of TALKING APES, void of IN-
TELLECT!!!!! *incapable* of LEARNING, &c.

tle children, and ourselves, and strip and beat us
one before the other—chain, hand-cuff, and drag us
about like rattle-snakes—shoot us down like wild
bears, before each other's faces, to make us submissive to, and work to support them and their families.
They (the whites) know well, if we are *men*—and
there is a secret monitor in their hearts which tells
them we are—they know, I say, if we *are* men,
and see them treating us in the manner they do,
that there can be nothing in our hearts but death
alone, for them , notwithstanding we may appear
cheerful, when we see them murdering our dear
mothers and wives, because we cannot help ourselves.   Man, in all ages and all nations of the
earth, is the same.   Man is a peculiar creature—he
is the image of his God, though he may be subjected to the most wretched condition upon earth, yet
the spirit and feeling which constitute the creature,
man, can never be entirely erased from his breast,
because the God who made him after his own image,
planted it in his heart; he cannot get rid of it. The
whites knowing this, they do not know what to do ;
they know that they have done us so much injury,
they are afraid that we, being men, and not brutes,
will retaliate, and woe will be to them ; therefore, that dreadful fear, together with an avaricious
spirit, and the natural love in them, to be called
masters, (which term will yet honour them with
to their sorrow) bring them to the resolve that they
will keep us in ignorance and wretchedness, as long
as they possibly can,* and make the best of their

---

* And still hold us up with indignity as being incapable of acquir-
ing knowledge ! ! ! See the inconsistency of the assertions of those
wretches—they beat us inhumanely, sometimes almost to death, for
attempting to inform ourselves, by reading the *Word* of our Maker,
and at the same time tell us, that we are beings *void of intellect! ! ! !*
How admirably their practices agree with their professions in this
case.   Let me cry shame upon you Americans, for such outrages
upon human nature ! ! ! If it were possible for the whites always
to keep us ignorant and miserable, and make us work to enrich
them and their children, and insult our feelings by representing us

time, while it lasts. Consequently they, themselves,
(and not us) render themselves our natural enemies,
by treating us so cruel. They keep us miserable
now, and call us their property, but some of them
will have enough of us by and by—their stomachs
shall run over with us; they want us for their slaves,
and shall have us to their fill. (We are all in the
world together ! !—I said above, because we cannot
help ourselves, (viz. we cannot help the whites
murdering our mothers and our wives) but this state-
ment is incorrect—for we can help ourselves; for,
if we lay aside abject servility, and be determined
to act like men, and not brutes—the murders among
the whites would be afraid to show their cruel heads.
But O, my God !—in sorrow I must say it, that my
colour, all over the world, have a mean, servile
spirit.   They yield in a moment to the whites, let
them be right or wrong—-the reason they are
able to keep their feet on our throats.   Oh ! my
coloured brethren, all over the world, when shall
we arise from this death-like apathy ?–And be men ! !
You will notice, if ever we become men, I mean
respectable men, such as other people are,) we must
exert ourselves to the full.   For remember, that it
is the greatest desire and object of the greater part
of the whites, to keep us ignorant, and make us work
to support them and their families.—Here now, in
the Southern and Western sections of this country,
there are at least three coloured persons for one
white, why is it, that those few weak, good-for-noth-
ing whites, are able to keep so many able men, one
of whom, can put to flight a dozen whites, in wretchedness and misery ?   It shows at once, what the
blacks are, we are ignorant, abject, servile and
mean—-and the whites know it—they know that we

---

as *talking Apes*, what would they do ?   But glory, honour and
praise to Heaven's King, that the sons and daughters of Africa,
will, in spite of all the opposition of their enemies, stand forth in all
the dignity and glory that is granted by the Lord to his creature
man.

are too servile to assert our rights as men—or they would not fool with us as they do. Would they fool with any other people as they do with us? No, they know too well, that they would get themselves ruined. Why do they not bring the inhabitants of Asia to be body servants to them? They know they would get their bodies rent and torn from head to foot. Why do they not get the Aborigines of this country to be slaves to them and their children, to work their farms and dig their mines? They know well that the Aborigines of this country, or (Indians) would tear them from the earth. The Indians would not rest day or night, they would be up all times of night, cutting their cruel throats. But my colour, (some, not all,) are willing to stand still and be murdered by the cruel whites. In some of the West-India Islands, and over a large part of South America, there are six or eight coloured persons for one white.* Why do they not take possession of those

---

* For instance in the two States of Georgia, and South Carolina, there are, perhaps, not much short of six or seven hundred thousand persons of colour; and if I was a gambling character, I would not be afraid to stake down upon the board Five Cents against Ten, that there are in the single State of Virginia, five or six hundred thousand Coloured persons. Four hundred and fifty thousand of whom (let them be well equipt for war) I would put against every white person on the whole continent of America. (Why? why because I know that the Blacks, once they get involved in a war, had rather die than to live, they either kill or be killed.) The whites know this too, which make them quake and tremble. To show the world further, how servile the coloured people are, I will only hold up to view, the one Island of Jamaica, as a specimen of our meanness.

In that Island, there are three hundred and fifty thousand souls —of whom fifteen thousand are whites, the remainder, three hundred and thirty-five thousand are coloured people! and this Island is ruled by the white people ! ! ! ! ! ! ! ! (15,000) ruling and tyranizing over 335,000 persons ! ! ! ! ! ! ! ! !—O! coloured men ! ! O! coloured men ! ! ! O! coloured men ! ! ! ! Look ! ! look ! ! ! at this ! ! ! ! and, tell me if we are not abject and servile enough, how long, O ! how long my colour shall we be dupes and dogs to the cruel whites ?—I only passed Jamaica, and its inhabitants, in review as a specimen to show the world, the condition of the Blacks at this time, now coloured people of the whole world, I beg you to look at the

places? Who hinders them? It is not the avaricious whites—for they are too busily engaged in laying up money—derived from the blood and tears of the blacks. The fact is, they are too servile, they love to have Masters too well!! Some of our brethren, too, who seeking more after self aggrandisement, than the glory of God, and the welfare of their brethren, join in with our oppressors, to ridicule and say all manner of evils falsely against our Bishop. They think, that they are doing great things, when they can get in company with the whites, to ridicule and make sport of those who are labouring for their good. Poor ignorant creatures, they do not know that the sole aim and object of the whites, are only to make fools and slaves of them, and put the whip to them, and make them work to support them and their families. But I do say, that no man, can well be a despiser of Bishop Allen, for his public labours among us, unless he is a despiser of God and of Righteousness. Thus, we see, my brethren, the two very opposite positions of those great men, who have written respecting this "Colonizing Plan." (Mr. Clay and his slave-holding party,) men who are resolved to keep us in eternal wretchedness, are also bent upon sending us to Liberia. While the Reverend Bishop Allen, and his party, men who have the fear of God, and the wellfare of their brethren at heart. The Bishop, in particular, whose labours for the salvation of his brethren, are well known to a large part of those, who dwell in the United States, are completely opposed to the plan—and advise us to stay where we are.

(15000 white,) and (Three Hundred and Thirty-five Thousand coloured people) in that Island, and tell me how can the white tyrants of the world but say that we are not men, but were made to be slaves and Dogs to them and their children forever !!!!!!!—why my friends only look at the thing !!!! (15000) whites keeping in wretchedness and degradation (335000) viz. 22 coloured persons for one white !!!!!!!!) when at the same time, an equal number (15000) Blacks, would almost take the whole of South America, because where they go as soldiers to fight death follows in their train.

Now we have to determine whose advice we will take respecting this all important matter, whether we will adhere to Mr. Clay and his slave holding party, who have always been our oppressors and murderers, and who are for colonizing us, more through apprehension than humanity, or to this godly man who has done so much for our benefit, together with the advice of all the good and wise among us and the whites. Will any of us leave our homes and go to Africa? I hope not.* Let them commence their attack upon us as they did on our brethren in Ohio, driving and beating us from our country, and my soul for theirs, they will have enough of it. Let no man of us budge one step, and let slave-holders come to beat us from our country. America is more our country, than it is the whites—we have enriched it with our *blood and tears.* The greatest riches in all America have arisen from our blood and tears :—and will they drive us from our property and homes, which we have earned with our *blood?* They must look sharp or this very thing will bring swift destruction upon them. The Americans have got so fat on our blood and groans, that they have almost forgotten the God of armies. But let them go on.

☞ ADDITION.—I will give here a very imperfect list of the cruelties inflicted on us by the enlightened Christians of America.—First, no trifling portion of them will beat us nearly to death, if they find us on our knees praying to God,—They hinder us from going to hear the word of God—they keep us sunk in ignorance, and will not let us learn to read the word of God, nor write—If they find us with a book of any description in our hand, they will beat us nearly to death—they are so afraid we will learn to read, and enlighten our dark and benighted minds

---

* Those who are ignorant enough to go to Africa, the coloured people ought to be glad to have them go, for if they are ignorant enough to let the whites *fool* them off to Africa, they would be no small injury to us if they reside in this country.

—They will not suffer us to meet together to worship the God who made us—they brand us with hot
iron—they cram bolts of fire down our throats—
they cut us as they do horses, bulls, or hogs—they
crop our ears and sometimes cut off bits of our
tongues—they chain and hand-cuff us, and while in
that miserable and wretched condition, beat us with
cow-hides and clubs—they keep us half naked and
starve us sometimes nearly to death under their infernal whips or lashes (which some of them shall
have enough of yet)—They put on us fifty-sixes
and chains, and make us work in that cruel situation, and in sickness, under lashes to support them
and their families.—They keep us three or four
hundred feet under ground working in their mines,
night and day to dig up gold and silver to enrich
them and their children.—They keep us in the
most death-like ignorance by keeping us from all
source of information, and call us, who are free men
and next to the Angels of God, their property ! ! ! ! ! !
They make us fight and murder each other, many
of us being ignorant, not knowing any better.—
They take us, (being ignorant,) and put us as drivers
one over the other, and make us afflict each other
as bad as they themselves afflict us—and to crown
the whole of this catalogue of cruelties, they tell us
that we the (blacks) are an inferior race of beings !
incapable of self government ! !—We would be injurious to society and ourselves, if tyrants should
loose their unjust hold on us ! ! ! That if we were
free we would not work, but would live on plunder
or theft ! ! ! ! that we are the meanest and laziest
set of beings in the world ! ! ! ! ! That they are obliged to keep us in bondage to do us good ! ! ! ! ! !—
That we are satisfied to rest in slavery to them and
their children ! ! ! ! ! !—That we ought not to be set
free in America, but ought to be sent away to Africa ! ! ! ! ! ! ! !—That if we were set free in America, we would involve the country in a civil war,
which assertion is altogether at variance with our

feeling or design, for we ask them for nothing but
the rights of man, viz. for them to set us free, and
treat us like men, and there will be no danger, for
we will love and respect them, and protect our
country—but cannot conscientiously do these things
until they treat us like men. 🔮

How cunning slave-holders think they are ! ! !—
How much like the king of Egyptwho, after he saw
plainly that God was determined to bring out his
people, in spite of him and his, as powerful as
they were. He was willing that Moses, Aaron and
the Elders of Israel, but not all the people should go
and serve the Lord. But God deceived him as he
will Christian Americans, unless they are very cau-
tious how they move. What would have become of
the United States of America, was it not for those
among the whites, who not in words barely, but
in truth and in deed, love and fear the Lord ?—
Our Lord and Master said :—† " Whoso shall of-
" fend one of these little ones which believe in me,
" it were better for him that a millstone were hang-
" ed about his neck, and that he were drowned in
" the depth of the sea." But the Americans with
this very threatening of the Lord's, not only beat
his little ones among the Africans, but many of them
they put to death or murder. Now the avaricious
Americans, think that the Lord Jesus Christ will
let them off, because his words are no more than
the words of a man ! ! ! In fact, many of them are
so avaricious and ignorant, that they do not believe
in our Lord and Saviour Jesus Christ. Tyrants
may think they are so skillful in State affairs is the
reason that the government is preserved. But I
tell you, that this country would have been given
up long ago, was it not for the lovers of the Lord.
They are indeed, the salt of the earth. Remove
the people of God among the whites, from this land
of blood, and it will stand until they cleverly get out
of the way.

---

* See St. Matthew's Gospel, chap. xviii. 6.

I adopt the language of the Rev. Mr. S. E. Cor-
nish, of New York, editor of the Rights of All, and
say : " Any coloured man of common intelligence,
" who gives his countenance and influence to that
" colony, further than its missionary object and in-
" interest extend, should be considered as a traitor
" to his brethren, and discarded by every respecta-
" ble man of colour. And every member of that
" society, however pure his motive, whatever may
" be his religious character and moral worth, should
" in his efforts to remove the coloured population
" from their rightful soil, the land of their birth and
" nativity, be considered as acting gratuitously un-
" righteous and cruel."

Let me make an appeal brethren, to your hearts,
for your cordial co-operation in the circulation of
" The Rights of All," among us. The utility of
such a vehicle if rightly conducted, cannot be esti-
mated. I hope that the well informed among us,
may see the absolute necessity of their co-operation
in its universal spread among us. If we should let
it go down, never let us undertake any thing of the
kind again, but give up at once and say that we are
really so ignorant and wretched that we cannot do
any thing at all!!—As far as I have seen the writings of its editor, I believe he is not seeking to fill
his pockets with money, but has the welfare of his
brethren truly at heart. Such men, brethren, ought
to be supported by us.

But to return to the colonizing trick. It will be
well for me to notice here at once, that I do not
mean indiscriminately to condemn all the members
and advocates of this scheme, for I believe that there
are some friends to the sons of Africa, who are labor-
ing for our salvation, not in words only but in truth
and in deed, who have been drawn into this plan.—
Some, more by persuasion than any thing else ;
while others, with humane feelings and lively zeal
for our good, seeing how much we suffer from the
afflictions poured upon us by unmerciful tyrants,

are willing to enroll their names in any thing which they think has for its ultimate end our redemption from wretchedness and miseries ; such men, with a heart truly overflowing with gratitude for their past services and zeal in our cause, I humbly beg to examine this plot minutely, and see if the end which they have in view will be completely consummated by such a course of procedure. Our friends who have been imperceptibly drawn into this plot I view with tenderness, and would not for the world injure their feelings, and I have only to hope for the future, that they will withdraw themselves from it ;— for I declare to them, that the plot is not for the glory of God, but on the contrary the perpetuation of slavery in this country, which will ruin them and the country forever, unless something is immediately done.

Do the colonizationists think to send us off without first being reconciled to us ? Do they think to bundle us up like brutes and send us off, as they did our brethren of the State of Ohio ?* Have they not to be reconciled to us, or reconcile us to them, for the cruelties with which they have afflicted our fathers and us? Methinks colonizationists think they have a set of brutes to deal with, sure enough. Do they think to drive us from our country and homes, after having enriched it with our blood and tears, and keep back millions of our dear brethren, sunk in the most barbarous wretchedness, to dig up gold and silver for them and their children? Surely, the Americans must think that we are brutes, as some

---

* The great slave holder, Mr. John Randolph, of Virginia, intimated in one of his *great, happy* and *eloquent* HARRANGUES, before the Virginia Convention, that Ohio is a slave State, by ranking it among other Slave-holding States. This probably was done by the HONORABLE *Slave-holder* to deter the minds of the ignorant ; to such I would say, that Ohio always was and is now a free State, that it never was and I do not believe it ever will be a Slave-holding State ; the people I believe, though some of them are hard hearted enough, detest Slavery too much to admit an evil into their bosom, which gnaws into the very vitals, and sinews of those who are now in possession of it.

of them have represented us to be. They think that
we do not feel for our brethren, whom they are murdering by the inches, but they are dreadfully deceived. I acknowledge that there are some deceitful and hypocritical wretches among us, who will
tell us one thing while they mean another, and thus
they go on aiding our enemies to oppress themselves
and us. But I declare this day before my Lord and
Master, that I believe there are some true-hearted
sons of Africa, in this land of oppression, but pretended *liberty ! ! ! !*—who do in reality feel for their
suffering brethren, who are held in bondage by tyrants. Some of the advocates of this cunningly de-
vised plot of Satan represent us to be the greatest
set of cut-throats in the world, as though God wants
us to take his work out of his hand before he is ready.
Does not vengeance belong to the Lord? Is he
not able to repay the Americans for their cruelties,
with which they have afflicted Africa's sons and
daughters, without our interference, unless we are
ordered? It is surprising to think that the Americans, having the Bible in their hands, do not believe
it. Are not the hearts of all men in the hands of
the God of battles? And does he not suffer some,
in consequence of cruelties, to go on until they are
irrecoverably lost? Now, what can be more aggravating, than for the Americans, after having treated
us so bad, to hold us up to the world as such great
throat-cutters? It appears to me as though they
are resolved to assail us with every species of afflic-
tion that their ingenuity can invent. ☞ See the
African Repository and Colonial Journal, from its
commencement to the present day—see how we are
through the medium of that periodical, abused and
held up by the Americans, as the greatest nuisance
to society, and throat-cutters in the world.) But the
Lord sees their actions. Americans! notwithstanding you have and do continue to treat us more cruel
than any heathen nation ever did a people it had subjected to the same condition that you have us. Now

let us reason—I mean you of the United States, whom I believe God designs to save from destruction, if you will hear. For I declare to you, whether you believe it or not, that there are some on the continent of America, who will never be able to repent. God will surely destroy them, to show you his disapprobation of the murders they and you have inflicted on us. I say, let us reason; had you not better take our body, while you have it in your power, and while we are yet ignorant and wretched, not knowing but a little, give us education, and teach us the pure religion of our Lord and Master, which is calculated to make the lion lay down in peace with the lamb, and which millions of you have beaten us nearly to death for trying to obtain since we have been among you, and thus at once, gain our affection while we are ignorant? Remember Americans, that we must and shall be free and enlightened as you are, will you wait until we shall, under God, obtain our liberty by the crushing arm of power? Will it not be dreadful for you? I speak Americans for your good. We must and shall be free I say, in spite of you. You may do your best to keep us in wretchedness and misery, to enrich you and your children, but God will deliver us from under you. And wo, wo, will be to you if we have to obtain our freedom by fighting. Throw away your fears and prejudices then, and enlighten us and treat us like men, and we will like you more than we do now hate you,* and tell us now no more about colonization, for America is as much our country, as it is yours.—Treat us like men, and there is no danger but we will all live in peace and happiness together. For we are not like you, hard hearted, unmerciful, and unforgiving. What a happy country this will be, if the whites will listen. What nation under heaven, will be able to do any thing with us, unless God gives us up into its hand? But Ameri-

---

* You are not astonished at my saying we hate you, for if we are men, we cannot but hate you, while you are treating us like dogs.

cans, I declare to you, while you keep us and our
children in bondage, and treat us like brutes, to
make us support you and your families, we cannot
be your friends. You do not look for it, do you?
Treat us then like men, and we will be your friends.
And there is not a doubt in my mind, but that the
whole of the past will be sunk into oblivion, and
we yet, under God, will become a united and happy people. The whites may say it is impossible,
but remember that nothing is impossible with God.

The Americans may say or do as they please, but
they have to raise us from the condition of brutes
to that of respectable men, and to make a national
acknowledgement to us for the wrongs they have
inflicted on us. As unexpected, strange, and wild
as these propositions may to some appear, it is no
less a fact, that unless they are complied with, the
Americans of the United States, though they may
for a little while escape, God will yet weigh them
in a balance, and if they are not superior to other
men, as they have represented themselves to be, he
will give them wretchedness to their very heart's
content.

And now brethren, having concluded these four
Articles, I submit them, together with my Preamble,
dedicated to the Lord, for your inspection, in language so very simple, that the most ignorant, who
can read at all, may easily understand—-of which
you may make the best you possibly can.* Should

---

* Some of my brethren, who are sensible, do not take an interest
in enlightening the minds of our more ignorant brethren respecting
this Book, and in reading it to them, just as though they will not
have either to stand or fall by what is written in this book. Do they
believe that I would be so foolish as to put out a book of this kind
without strict—ah! very strict commandments of the Lord?—Surely the blacks and whites must think that I am ignorant enough.—
Do they think that I would have the audacious wickedness to take
the name of my God in vain?

Notice, I said in the concluding clause of Article 3—I call God,
I call Angels, I call men to witness, that the destruction of the
Americans is at hand, and will be speedily consummated unless they
repent. Now I wonder if the world think that I would take the

tyrants take it into their heads to emancipate any of
you, remember that your freedom is your natural
right. You are men, as well as they, and instead
of returning thanks to them for your freedom, return it to the Holy Ghost, who is our rightful own-
er. If they do not want to part with your labours,
which have enriched them, let them keep you, and
my word for it, that God Almighty, will break their
strong band. Do you believe this, my brethren?—
See my Address, delivered before the General Coloured Association of Massachusetts, which may be
found in Freedom's Journal, for Dec. 20, 1828.—
See the last clause of that Address. Whether you
believe it or not, I tell you that God will dash tyrants, in combination with devils, into atoms, and
will bring you out from your wretchedness and miseries under these *Christian People! ! ! ! ! !*

Those philanthropists and lovers of the human
family, who have volunteered their services for our
redemption from wretchedness, have a high claim
on our gratitude, and we should always view them
as our greatest earthly benefactors.

If any are anxious to ascertain who I am, know
the world, that I am one of the oppressed, degraded
and wretched sons of Africa, rendered so by the
avaricious and unmerciful, among the whites.—If
any wish to plunge me into the wretched incapaci-
ty of a slave, or murder me for the truth, know ye,
that I am in the hand of God, and at your disposal.
I count my life not dear unto me, but I am ready
to be offered at any moment. For what is the use
of living, when in fact I am dead. But remember,
Americans, that as miserable, wretched, degraded
and abject as you have made us in preceding, and
in this generation, to support you and your families,

name of God in this way in vain? What do they think I take God
to be? Do they suppose that I would trifle with that God who will
not have his Holy name taken in vain?—He will show you and the
world, in due time, whether this book is for his glory, or written by
me through envy to the whites. as some have represented.

11

that some of you, (whites) on the continent of America, will yet curse the day that you ever were born. You want slaves, and want us for your slaves !!! My colour will yet, root some of you out of the very face of the earth !!!!!! You may doubt it if you please. I know that thousands will doubt—they think they have us so well secured in wretchedness, to them and their children, that it is impossible for such things to occur.* So did the antideluvians doubt

---

* Why do the Slave-holders or Tyrants of America and their advocates fight so hard to keep my brethren from receiving and reading my Book of Appeal to them?—Is it because they treat us so well?—Is it because we are satisfied to rest in Slavery to them and their children?—Is is because they are treating us like men, by compensating us all over this free country ! ! for our labours?—But why are the Americans so very fearfully terrified respecting my Book?—Why do they search vessels, &c. when entering the harbours of tyrannical States, to see if any of my Books can be found, for fear that my brethren will get them to read. Why, I thought the Americans proclaimed to the world that they are a happy, enlightened, humane and Christian people, all the inhabitants of the country enjoy equal Rights ! ! America is the Asylum for the oppressed of all nations !!!

Now I ask the Americans to see the fearful terror they labor under for fear that my brethren will get my Book and read it—and tell me if their declaration is true—viz. if the United States of America is a Republican Government?—Is this not the most tyrannical, unmerciful, and cruel government under Heaven?—not excepting the Algerines, Turks and Arabs ?—I believe if any candid person would take the trouble to go through the Southern and Western sections of this country, and could have the heart to see the cruelties inflicted by these *Christians* on us, he would say, that the Algerines, Turks and Arabs treat their dogs a thousand times better than we are treated by the *Christians*.—But perhaps the Americans do their very best to keep my Brethren from receiving and reading my "Appeal" for fear they will find in it an extract which I made from their Declaration of Independence, which says, "we hold these truths to be self-evident, that all men are created equal," &c. &c. &c.—If the above are not the causes of the alarm among the Americans, respecting my Book, I do not know what to impute it to, unless they are possessed of the same spirit with which Demetrius the Silversmith was possessed—however, that they may judge whether they are of the same avaricious and ungodly spirit with that man, I will give here an extract from the Acts of the Apostles, chapter xix.—verses 23, 24, 25, 26, 27.

" And the same time there arose no small stir about that way. For a cer-
" tain *man* named Demetrius, a silversmith, which made silver shrines for
" Diana, brought no small gain unto the craftsmen ; whom he called together
" with the workmen of like occupation, and said, Sirs, ye know that by this
" craft we have our wealth: moreover, ye see and hear, that not alone at
" Ephesus, but almost throughout all Asia, this Paul hath persuaded and turn-
" ed away much people, saying, that they be no gods which are made with
" hands : so that not only this our craft is in danger to be set at nought ; but
" also that the temple of the great goddess Diana should be despised, and her
" magnificence should be destroyed, whom all Asia and the world worship-
" peth."

I pray you Americans of North and South America, together with the whole European inhabitants of the world, (I mean Slave-holders and their advocates) to read and ponder over the above verses in your minds, and judge whether or not you are of the infernal spirit with that Heathen Demetrius, the Silversmith: In fine I beg you to read the whole chapter through carefully.

Noah, until the day in which the flood came and swept them away. So did the Sodomites doubt, until Lot had got out of the city, and God rained down fire and brimstone from Heaven upon them, and burnt them up. So did the king of Egypt doubt the very existence of a God; he said, "who is the Lord, that I should let Israel go?" Did he not find to his sorrow, who the Lord was, when he and all his mighty men of war, were smothered to death in the Red Sea? So did the Romans doubt, many of them were really so ignorant, that they thought the whole of mankind were made to be slaves to them; just as many of the Americans think now, of my colour. But they got dreadfully deceived. When men got their eyes opened, they made the murderers scamper. The way in which they cut their tyrannical throats, was not much inferior to the way the Romans or murderers, served them, when they held them in wretchedness and degradation under their feet. So would Christian Americans doubt, if God should send an Angel from Heaven to preach their funeral sermon. The fact is, the Christians having a name to live, while they are dead, think that God will screen them on that ground.

See the hundreds and thousands of us that are thrown into the seas by Christians, and murdered by them in other ways. They cram us into their vessel holds in chains and in hand-cuffs—men, women and children, all together!! O! save us, we pray thee, thou God of Heaven and of earth, from the devouring hands of the white Christians!!!

Oh! thou Alpha and Omega!
The beginning and the end,
Enthron'd thou art, in Heaven above,
Surrounded by Angels there:

From whence thou seest the miseries
To which we are subject;
The whites have murder'd us, O God!
And kept us ignorant of thee.

Not satisfied with this, my Lord !
They throw us in the seas :
Be pleas'd, we pray, for Jesus' sake,
To save us from their grasp.

We believe that, for thy glory's sake,
Thou wilt deliver us ;
But that thou may'st effect these things,
Thy glory must be sought.

In conclusion, I ask the candid and unprejudiced of the whole world, to search the pages of historians diligently, and see if the Antideluvians—the Sodomites—the Egyptians—the Babylonians—the Ninevites—the Carthagenians—the Persians—the Macedonians—the Greeks—the Romans—the Mahometans—the Jews—or devils, ever treated a set of human beings, as the white Christians of America do us, the blacks, or Africans. I also ask the attention of the world of mankind to the declaration of these very American people, of the United States.

A declaration made July 4, 1776.

It says, *" When in the course of human events, " it becomes necessary for one people to dissolve " the political bands which have connected them " with another, and to assume among the Powers of " the earth, the separate and equal station to which "the laws of nature and of nature's God entitle " them. A decent respect for the opinions of mankind " requires, that they should declare the causes which " impel them to the separation.—We hold these " truths to be self evident—that all men are created " equal, that they are endowed by their Creator " with certain unalienable rights: that among these, " are life, liberty, and the pursuit of happiness that, " to secure these rights, governments are instituted " among men, deriving their just powers from the

* See the Declaration of Independence of the United States.

" consent of the governed ; that when ever any form
" of government becomes destructive of these ends, it
" is the right of the people to alter or to abolish it,
" and to institute a new government laying its
" foundation on such principles, and organizing its
" powers in such form, as to them shall seem most
" likely to effect their safety and happiness. Pru-
" dence, indeed, will dictate, that governments long
" established should not be changed for light and
" transient causes ; and accordingly all experience
" hath shewn, that mankind are more disposed to
" suffer, while evils are sufferable, than to right
" themselves by abolishing the forms to which they
" are accustomed. But when a long train of abu-
" ses and usurpations, pursuing invariably the same
" object, evinces a design to reduce them under abso-
" lute despotism, it is their right it is their duty to
" throw off such government, and to provide new
" guards for their future security." See your Declaration Americans ! ! ! Do you understand your
own language? Hear your language, proclaimed
to the world, July 4th, 1776—☞ " We hold these
" truths to be self evident—that ALL MEN ARE
" CREATED EQUAL !! that they *are endowed by*
" *their Creator with certain unalienable rights ;* that
" among these are life, *liberty,* and the pursuit of
" happiness ! !" Compare your own language
above, extracted from your Declaration of Independence, with your cruelties and murders inflicted by your cruel and unmerciful fathers and
yourselves on our fathers and on us—men who have
never given your fathers or you the least provocation ! ! ! ! !

Hear your language further ! ☞ " But when a
" long train of abuses and usurpation, pursuing
" invariably the same object, evinces a design to re-
" duce them under absolute despotism, it is their
" *right,* it is their *duty,* to throw off such govern-
" ment, and to provide new guards for their future
" security."

Now, Americans! I ask you candidly, was your sufferings under Great Britain, one hundredth part as cruel and tyranical as you have rendered ours under you? Some of you, no doubt, believe that we will never throw off your murderous government and "provide new guards for our future security." If Satan has made you believe it, will he not deceive you?* Do the whites say, I being a black man, ought to be humble, which I readily admit? I ask them, ought they not to be as humble as I? or do they think that they can measure arms with Jehovah? Will not the Lord yet humble them? or will not these very coloured people whom they now treat worse than brutes, yet under God, humble them low down enough? Some of the whites are ignorant enough to tell us, that we ought to be submissive to them, that they may keep their feet on our throats. And if we do not submit to be beaten to death by them, we are bad creatures and of course must be damned, &c. If any man wishes to hear this doctrine openly preached to us by the American preachers, let him go into the Southern and Western sections of this country—I do not speak from hear say—what I have written, is what I have seen and heard myself. No man may think that my book is made up of conjecture—I have travelled and observed nearly the whole of those things myself, and what little I did not get by my own observation, I received from those among the whites and blacks, in whom the greatest confidence may be placed.

The Americans may be as vigilant as they please, but they cannot be vigilant enough for the Lord, neither can they hide themselves, where he will not find and bring them out.

---

* The Lord has not taught the Americans that we will not some day or other throw off their chains and hand-cuffs, from our hands and feet, and their devilish lashes (which some of them shall have enough of yet) from off our backs.

1 Thy presence why withdraw'st, Lord ?
    Why hid'st thou now thy face,
When dismal times of deep distress
    Call for thy wonted grace ?

2 The wicked, swell'd with lawless pride,
    Have made the poor their prey ;
O let them fall by those designs
    Which they for others lay.

3 For straight they triumph, if success
    Their thriving crimes attend ;
And sordid wretches, whom God hates,
    Perversely they command.

4. To own a pow'r above themselves
    Their haughty pride disdains ;
And, therefore, in their stubborn mind
    No thought of God remains.

5 Oppressive methods they pursue,
    And all their foes they slight ;
Because thy judgments, unobserv'd,
    Are far above their sight.

6 They fondly think their prosp'rous state
    Shall unmolested be ;
They think their vain designed shall thrive,
    From all misfortune free.

7 Vain and deceitful is their speech,
    With curses fill'd, and lies ;
By which the mischief of their heart
    They study to disguise.

8 Near public roads they lie conceal'd
    And all their art employ,
The innocent and poor at once
    To rifle and destroy.

9 Not lions, crouching in their dens,
    Surprise their heedless prey
With greater cunning, or express
    More savage rage than they.

10 Sometimes they act the harmless man,
    And modest looks they wear ;
That so, deceiv'd the poor may less
    Their sudden onset fear.

PART II.

11. For, God, they think, no notice takes,
    Of their unrighteous deeds;
He never minds the suff'ring poor,
    Nor their oppression heeds.

12. But thou, O Lord, at length arise,
    Stretch forth thy mighty arm,
And, by the greatness of thy pow'r,
    Defend the poor from harm.

13 No longer let the wicked vaunt,
    And, proudly boasting, say,
  " Tush, God regards not what we do ;
  " He never will repay."—*Common Prayer Book.*

1 Shall I for fear of feeble man,
The spirit's course in me restrain ?
Or, undismay'd in deed and word,
Be a true witness of my Lord.

2 Aw'd by mortal's frown, shall I
Conceal the word of God Most High !
How then before thee shall I dare
To stand, or how thy anger bear ?

3 Shall I, to soothe th' unholy throng,
Soften the truth, or smooth my tongue,
To gain earth's gilded toys or, flee
The cross endur'd, my Lord, by thee ?

4 What then is he whose scorn I dread ?
Whose wrath or hate makes me afraid
A man ! an heir of death ! a slave
To sin ! a bubble on the wave !

5 Yea, let men rage, since thou will spread
Thy shadowing wings around my head :
Since in all pain thy tender love
Will still my sure refreshment prove.

                        Wesleys Collection.

☞ It may not be understood, when I say my Third and last Edition, I mean to convey the idea, that there will be no more Books of this Third Edition printed, but to notify that there will be no more addition in the body of this Work, or additional Notes to this " Appeal."☜

                THE END.

CPSIA information can be obtained
at www.ICGtesting.com
Printed in the USA
BVHW081046210819
556415BV00004B/455/P